Studies in
Major Literary Authors

edited by
William Cain
Wellesley College

A Routledge Series

OTHER BOOKS IN THIS SERIES:

THE WAYWARD NUN
OF AMHERST
*Emily Dickinson in the Medieval
Women's Visionary Tradition*
by Angela Conrad

PHILIP ROTH CONSIDERED
*The Concentrationary Universe
of the American Writer*
by Steven Milowitz

THE PUSHER AND THE SUFFERER
*An Unsentimental Reading of
Moby Dick*
by Suzanne Stein

HENRY JAMES AS A BIOGRAPHER
A Self Among Others
by Willie Tolliver

JOYCEAN FRAMES
Film and the Fiction of James Joyce

Thomas L. Burkdall

ROUTLEDGE
A MEMBER OF THE TAYLOR & FRANCIS GROUP
NEW YORK & LONDON/2001

Published in 2001 by
Routledge
A member of the Taylor & Francis Group
29 West 35th Street
New York, NY 10001

Copyright © 2001 by Thomas L. Burkdall

All rights reserved. No part of this book may be reprinted or reproduced or utilized in any form or by any electronic, mechanical, or other means, now known or hereafter invented, including photocopying and recording, or in any information storage or retrieval system, without written permission from the publishers.

10 9 8 7 6 5 4 3 2 1

Library of Congress Cataloging-in-Publication Data is available from the Library of Congress.

ISBN 0-8153-3928-3

To Lisa,

first and ever.

Contents

Acknowledgments	ix
The Direct Attack: An Introduction	xi
Chapter One—The Unknown Art: Joyce and Cinema	1
Chapter Two—The New Fashionable Kinematographic Vein	19
Chapter Three—Bioscope: Portraits of Reality	31
Chapter Four—In the Linguistic Kitchen: Joyce, Eisenstein and Cinema Language	49
Chapter Five—Cinema Fakes: Film and Joycean Fantasy	65
Chapter Six—A Look Between: A Cinematic Analysis of "Nausicaa"	81
Conclusion: From Film and Literature to Movies and Modernism	97
Bibliography	101
Index	111

Acknowledgments

Thank Movies from the innermost depths of my still attrite heart.

—*Finnegans Wake*, 194.2-3

The writing of any critical study involves many more individuals than its author alone; works about James Joyce and his fiction tend to be still more of a communal effort. Many friends and colleagues, teachers and counselors have assisted with this study and deserve my gratitude.

Thanks are due to James Harville and Bill Sullivan who introduced me to the works of Joyce under the watchful and tolerant eyes of the Jesuits. The late Beverle Houston would have recognized her influence in this study through the union of film history, aesthetics and theory alongside of literature and literary criticism; Ellin Ringler-Henderson, Barry Sanders and Albert Wachtel also may glimpse their personal imprints and the interdisciplinary nature of Pitzer College within these pages.

Through the course of my studies at UCLA, a number of Joyceans and modernists have aided me and deserve mention. In 1983, Jack Kolb planted the seed of this study, and with patience and skill, saw to it that the idea was nurtured. Through his courses, Calvin Bedient helped me to deepen my critical awareness and, by both example and commentary, taught me much about writing. Though always busy with his own career and family, Kevin Dettmar has watched me struggle with this project, never hesitating to lend assistance, knowledge and an ear.

Susan Brienza has since moved on to other endeavours, but her legacy at UCLA continued. Of all her numerous efforts to assist my scholarly development, none matches the commitment and drive which initiated and supported the Southern California *Finnegans Wake* Circle in its early years. This group not only sustained a local Joyce community, but has served as an invaluable connection to the national and international organizations as well. Through her efforts, I have been able to meet many scholars—without her, I might never have come to know Vincent Cheng of University of Southern California, ever gracious and generous, or Margot Norris of University of California, Irvine, an insightful and helpful woman. I wish to thank the Circle's ever-transforming membership for their Joycean fellowship and the formative influence they have had on my work and my professional development.

Leaving UCLA, I had the good fortune to study *Ulysses* with Michael Seidel of Columbia University and the wonderful group he invited there to participate in a National Endowment for the Humanities Seminar in the mild New York summer of 1992.

At Occidental College, Deborah Martinson with her knowledge of writing, modernism and feminism has aided me in many endeavours. Thanks are due to her for agreeing to read this study in a late draft and offer helpful suggestions.

Friends and family also contribute to a work such as this. The Richeys—Bill, Esther and Blanche—former neighbors and constant friends often provided support and diversion. Lucia, Erin and Zither have always listened and comforted frayed nerves. Rory, Conor and Paddy shared their enthusiasm for all things Irish. Don Burkdall, offered frequent support. From a distance and throughout the years, Roberta and Oscar Rambeau helped me to see the study to completion. And Lisa, who helped in all ways, can never be thanked enough.

INTRODUCTION
The Direct Attack

> And he sets his mind to work upon unknown arts and changes the laws of nature.
>
> —Ovid, Metamorphoses, VIII:188

Ovid's description of Dædalus' meditations, used in part as the epigraph to *A Portrait of the Artist as a Young Man,* applies to both fictional and actual artificers, not only to Stephen Dedalus but also to James Joyce. Whether in the classical or the modern eras, intertextuality extends far beyond the written word—rather, it suggests a transference of the means of signification between sign systems (Kristeva, 59–60). Such transposition between film and literature seemed inevitable to Leo Tolstoy as early as 1908:

> You will see that this little clicking contraption with the revolving handle will make a revolution in our life—in the life of writers. It is a direct attack on the old methods of literary art. We shall have to adapt ourselves to the shadowy screen and to the cold machine. A new form of writing will be necessary. I have thought of that and I can feel what is coming. (Spiegel, 162)

Joyce's writing represents the fulfillment of Tolstoy's prophecy. As Keith Cohen reminds us, the sign systems of literature and film approximate one another. Invoking Christian Metz, Cohen declares that "the relation between two sign systems, like novel and film" can be studied since "the same codes may reappear in more than one system" (3). Viewing Joyce's works by the flickering light of the early cinema and the theory of that art produces intriguing results.

The connection between Joyce's fiction and the cinema does not represent a new idea; the works of James Joyce have been called "cinematic" often enough to consider this pronouncement a critical commonplace. Even *Time*, with the hyperbole of journalism, dubbed James Joyce "movie crazy" (Spiegel, 72). And in a letter to the French film critic Léon Moussinac, Sergei Eisenstein declared that "what Joyce does in literature is quite near to what we do and even closer to what we have intentions of doing with the new cinematography" (120–121). Beyond the impressions of the news magazine and the proclamations of the great Russian film maker, biographical evidence confirms Joyce's commercial and aesthetic interest in film.

In one of the first full-length studies of the *oeuvre*, *James Joyce: A Critical Introduction*, Harry Levin maintains that in "its intimacy and in its continuity, *Ulysses* has more in common with the cinema than with other fiction" (88). While this claim may be an exaggeration, Levin proceeds to convincingly compare the style of *Ulysses* with that of a cinematic montage:

> Bloom's mind is neither *tabula rasa* nor a photographic plate, but a motion picture, which has been ingeniously cut and edited to emphasize the close-ups and fade-outs of flickering emotions, the angles of observation and the flashbacks of reminiscence. . . . The movement of Joyce's style, the thought of his characters is like unreeling film; his method of construction, the arrangement of this raw material, involves the crucial operation of montage. (88)

But what precisely, beyond the metaphor of montage, do we mean when we describe Joyce's work as "cinematic" and how do we discuss the cinematic qualities of a piece of literature? Specific films that influenced Joyce's writing will probably never be determined; we know of some films he saw, but he never spoke of them as inspirations for his writing. Joyce did acknowledge some impact of film upon his work, as I shall discuss in Chapter one; yet the paucity of direct evidence certainly limits such an approach. Another critical method might be to analyze the fiction in relation to cinematic techniques. But evaluating literature merely in terms of shot construction, superimposition and scenes is often dissatisfying and mechanical. If we may regard Joyce's fiction as "cinematic," the principles of film theory should apply to his works. By employing concepts from this discipline, the cinematic aspects of the works may be examined without making assumptions based upon scanty evidence or using a reductive methodology.

An analysis of Joyce's work, from *Dubliners* to *Finnegans Wake*, in light of both this relationship between sign systems and film theory will render new insights about his fiction. In my investigation, I not only document Joyce's biographical associations with the movies, I also consider the relationship of Joyce's modernist texts to the art and criticism of film and explore the relationship of the reader to the text. As Joyce's canon evolves, different aspects of film theory and practice bear relevance to his work. André Bazin's commentary on Italian neo-realism and Walther Ruttmann's *Berlin* shed light on the realistic aspects of *Dubliners* and *Ulysses*, while Sergei Eisenstein's essays aid in a discussion of montage and the deformation of images, characteristics that emerge in *A Portrait of the Artist as a Young Man*, only to blossom fully in the later works. I analyze the fantastic elements of the "Circe" episode of *Ulysses* and the techniques of *Finnegans Wake* in terms of Vachel Lindsay's early film criticism and compare them with the trick films of Méliès. Finally, I demonstrate how film theory illuminates Joyce's texts; an application of the feminist psychoanalytic concepts of Laura Mulvey and Mary Ann Doane offers insight into the manipulation of the gaze and the reinforcement of the patriarchal order in the "Nausicaa" episode. Such criticism further raises the issue of the reader's gender and his or her identification with the characters and the text.

Literary criticism in general, and Joyce criticism in particular, ought not to continue to ignore the relationship of this century's two most popular narrative art forms. Film has long acknowledged its literary debt; the time has now arrived for critics to examine the relationship of Joyce, a quintessential modernist, to his era's new art form. Furthermore, since critical works, such as Cheryl Herr's *Joyce's Anatomy of Culture* and R. B. Kershner's *Joyce, Bakhtin, and Popular Literature: Chronicles of Disorder*, have examined the presence and significance of popular culture in Joyce's work, it is time for an analysis of Joyce and cinema, a new and crucial media of his time.

The introductory chapter, "The Unknown Art: Joyce and Cinema" provides further biographical and critical justification for the study. In it, I first compile the evidence of Joyce's connections with film, drawing from letters and various other biographical sources. A review of the criticism concerning Joyce and the cinema follows this section, outlining the major approaches that such research has taken and considering the ways in which my study differs from previous work.

In the next chapter, "The New Fashionable Kinematographic

Vein," I consider film as a constructive influence on perception and understanding in two ways: 1) cinema as a mechanical art changes the perspective of both the spectator (using Walter Benjamin's "The Work of Art in the Age of Mechanical Reproduction") and the artist (with reference to Kenner's *The Mechanic Muse*) and 2) film as an idea serves as an appropriate metaphor for the mind's process in conjunction with the philosophy of Henri Bergson. A consideration of the era and the cinema's importance in it, using Arnold Hauser's chapter entitled "The Film Age" from *The Social History of Art,* conclude the chapter.

The first chapter to treat Joyce's fiction in detail, entitled "Bioscope: Portraits of Reality," concerns the realistic aspect of film. It treats the extraordinary precision of the camera and its potential influence upon the realistic novelist. I consider the early documentary pieces of the Lumières and others, and the work of Robert Flaherty and Walther Ruttmann, two directors mentioned in connection with the film adaptation of *Ulysses* proposed in the thirties. In addition to this consideration of film practice, I examine theories of cinematic/photographic realism, including those of Benedetto Croce and Susan Sontag. Finally, I apply the ideas expressed in André Bazin's essays on Italian Neorealism to *Dubliners*, illustrating the parallels in purpose and method between these two depictions of European life.

"In the Linguistic Kitchen: Joyce, Eisenstein and Cinema Language" discusses Eisenstein's theories of montage and their applicability to combinations of words, as well to the disproportion in representation, in *Dubliners, A Portrait of the Artist as a Young Man* and *Ulysses*. I bring to bear Eisenstein's brief observations regarding Joyce's art in examining the representation of the characters' psyches in the novels.

Using the "fantastic" elements of the films of Méliès as a starting point (as Austin Briggs suggests) and considering various non-cinematic sources, in "Cinema Fakes: Film and Joycean Fantasy" I discuss the protosurrealistic cinematic aspects of *Ulysses* and the cinematic analogues of the experimental nature of character and event in *Finnegans Wake*. I examine the swiftness of the grotesque transformations of the later chapters of *Ulysses* and aspects of *Finnegans Wake* in light of a film theorist and American poet contemporary to Joyce, Vachel Lindsay, who wrote of the artistic potentials of film in 1915.

In "A Look Between: A Cinematic Analysis of 'Nausicaa,'" the work of feminist film theorists Laura Mulvey (based in part on the ideas of Peter Berger and Lacanian psychoanalysis) and Mary Ann Doane (utilizing Joan Riviere's theory of masquerade in an attempt to define female spectatorship) provide the methodology for analyzing the voyeurism and scopophilia in this chapter of *Ulysses*. In examining the relationsship between watcher and watched, reader/spectator and character, these critics help to elucidate the sexual and visual elements of the novel and how it compares with the cinema.

CHAPTER ONE
The Unknown Art
Joyce and Cinema

> I see a cinematograph going on and on . . .
>
> —*Letters*, 27 June 1924

A substantial amount of biographical evidence confirms Joyce's interest in the cinema and encourages further investigation of his aesthetic affinities with film. A review of his connections with the movies throughout his life reveal both his opinions about films and his relationship to them—not only as spectator and artist, but also as entrepreneur and negotiator.

Two of Joyce's earliest writings suggest film technique. In these juvenilia, a cinematic means of representation is evident. One of the adolescent's *Silhouettes*, composed while Joyce attended Belvedere College, and recalled by Stanislaus Joyce in his reminiscence, *My Brother's Keeper*, is particularly evocative. Related in the first person, the narrator's

> attention is attracted by two figures in violent agitation on a lowered window-blind illuminated from within, the burly figure of a man, staggering and threatening with upraised fist, and the smaller sharp-faced figure of a nagging woman. A blow is struck and the light goes out. The narrator waits to see if anything happens afterwards. Yes, the window-blind is illuminated again dimly, by a candle no doubt, and the woman's sharp profile appears accompanied by two small heads, just above the window-ledge, of children wakened by the noise. The woman's finger is pointed in warning. She is saying, 'Don't waken Pa'. (90)

The domestic violence and mundane trauma of this early sketch presage the development of similar themes in *Dubliners*. But as Austin Briggs notes with respect to this piece, "even in his teens Joyce demonstrated an interest in projections upon screens" (145). And Homer Obed Brown points out that "a 'silhouette' emphasizes the externality of the description, frames the scene as if on a stage, and exaggerates its distance from the narrator. It presents the voyeuristic aspect of the detached observer in its simplest form" (21). But this narrator represents the voyeur within the film, coupled with the spectator of the movie house—the narrator looks on at the event related, while the audience identifies with this protagonist/teller whom we observe as he watches.[1]

In Joyce's first attempt at self-portraiture on January 7, 1904, he describes memory and the mind's images of the past in almost cinematic terms.[2] The opening paragraph of his essay, "A Portrait of the Artist," contains some language suggestive of film:

> The features of infancy are not commonly reproduced in the adolescent portrait for, so capricious are we, that we cannot or will not conceive the past in any other than its iron memorial aspect. Yet *the past assuredly implies a fluid succession of presents, the development of an entity of which our actual present is a phase only.* Our world, again, recognises its acquaintance chiefly by the characters of beard and inches and is, for the most part, estranged from those of its members who seek through some art, by some process of the mind yet untabulated, to liberate from the personalised lumps of matter that which is their individuating rhythm, the first or formal relation of their parts. But for such as these a portrait is not an identificative paper but rather the curve of an emotion. (Emphasis added, 257–58)

The "fluid succession of presents" describes aptly both the process and the product of the cinema, while the "individuating rhythm" reminds one not only of Stephen Dedalus's later Thomistic pronouncements, but also of the rhythm of montage. It resembles the sort of phrase that Sergei Eisenstein might have written to describe how montage captures the essence of an image through the relation of its parts. In rendering the "curve of an emotion" and by envisioning a calculus of affect, Joyce presages a literature analogous to Eisenstein's cinema of an "inner monologue," a form that the Russian director admires in prose fiction but which he believes "finds full expression ... only in the cinema" (*Film Form*, 104–05).

Two of Joyce's early explicit references to film suggest the impression it made upon him. Writing from Pola, in 1904 Joyce observed the power of the medium to enthrall audiences. He describes a memorable night at the cinema: "The other evening we went to a bioscope. There were a series of pictures about betrayed Gretchen. In the third last [act] Lothario throws her into the river and rushes off, followed by rabble. Nora said, 'O, policeman, catch him'" (*Letters* 2: 75). Two years later, in a letter to Stanislaus, Joyce compares the cinematograph with the mind's processes; at the end of a missive that changes topics so swiftly it might have been a futurist piece celebrating dynamism and Filippo Marinetti's god of speed, Joyce declares, "the Italian imagination is like a cinematograph, observe the style of my letter" (2: 203).

Although Joyce only occasionally writes of the cinema in his correspondence, he does reveal that he turned to the new medium for solace at a critical moment in his life. A troubled exile in Rome in 1907, Joyce confessed to his brother Stanislaus that:

> I have gradually slid down until I have ceased to take any interest in any subject. I look at God and his theatre through the eyes of my fellow-clerks so that nothing surprises, moves, excites or disgusts me. Nothing of my former mind seems to have remained except a heightened emotiveness which satisfies itself in the sixty-miles-an-hour pathos of some cinematograph or before some crude Italian gazette-picture.

But the cinema represented more than a place for Joyce to recapture his former mental and emotional state. In this particular epistle, he describes a writer's crisis of faith, a situation that serves to underscore the restorative powers of the cinematograph's emotional carousel. Joyce understands that he must decide now: "it is about time I made up my mind whether I am to become a writer or a patient Cousins." He suffers from "mental extinction" and "indifference," while lamenting the cultural and mental bankruptcy of his employers, the Roman bankers, and his fellow employees, tellers and clerks. Even the romanticism of Wagner's *Dusk of the Gods*, as Joyce refers to the opera, fails to cheer him. Discouraged by the problems of publishing *Dubliners*, even the proofs of *Chamber Music* cannot comfort him for long. By the end of the letter, he even suggests that "the verses are not worth talking about: and I begin to think neither are the stories." Alongside the temporary relief of his poems, the cinematograph is an unequivocal positive. (See *Letters*, 2: 217.)

However, the most obvious of the early connections between Joyce and the cinema may be more commercial than emotional or aesthetic. In one of his early business ventures, he attempted to establish the first movie-house in all of Ireland. The tenure of Ireland's first cinematograph manager was, fortunately for modern letters, both short and unsuccessful, lasting less than three months. Yet, this incident should not be dismissed as simply another of Joyce's entrepreneurial failures; while his plans to import fireworks or Irish tweed to Italy were soon forgotten (Ellmann, 303), Joyce retained an interest in film throughout his life. As Gösta Werner indicates, some of the mainly Italian films shown at the Volta Cinematograph reappear in Joyce's writings, especially in *Finnegans Wake* (132).

By the early 1920s Joyce clearly recognized the parallels between his own writing and the cinematic medium. As Ellmann notes, the author "at first . . . had thought, as he told [his friend] Daniel Hummel, that the book [*Ulysses*] could not be translated into another language, but might be translated into another medium, that of the film" (561). And, a little later, Joyce clarified the analogy between the mind and the cinema. Those "prolonged cinema nights" which Joyce mentioned to Harriet Shaw Weaver refer, as Ellmann remarks, to an earlier letter in which Joyce suggested how he viewed films in relation to consciousness and recollection (3: 112). "Whenever I am obliged to lie with my eyes closed," he writes, "I see a cinematograph going on and on and it brings back to my memory things I had almost forgotten," showing the link that Joyce discerned between his own stream-of-consciousness and the rapidly moving images of the cinema (1: 216).

In their reminiscences, his friends and acquaintances also document the author's interest in the movies; he attended the cinema often in Paris in the twenties. In an article in *Sight and Sound*, Patricia Hutchins describes his movie-going habits:

> In spite of increasing difficulties with his eyes, he appears to have gone fairly frequently to the movies, usually between dusk and dinner time when he could no longer work. Paul Léon or Joyce's son and daughter-in-law usually accompanied him. (11)

Joyce, the tired craftsman, relaxed in the darkness of the theater. But were these evening sojourns more than a pleasant pastime? Morley Callaghan, a Canadian novelist and acquaintance of Joyce in Paris, certainly thought so. He recalls one evening in his memoir of 1929,

The Unknown Art: Joyce and Cinema

That Summer in Paris:

> Joyce got talking about the movies. A number of times a week he went to the movies. Movies interested him. As he talked, I seemed to see him in a darkened theatre, the great prose master absorbed in camera technique, so like the dream technique, one picture then another flashing in the mind. Did it all add to his knowledge of the dream world? (142–43)

In a section of "Further Notes" to her study, *James Joyce's World*, Hutchins adds a few more pieces of information concerning Joyce and the cinema. Apparently Joyce told Harriet Shaw Weaver that he found the inspiration for the rhythm of Molly's soliloquy in "a film on astronomy, in particular some sequences dealing with the moon" (245). Eugene and Maria Jolas also tell of attending the cinema with Joyce, remembering that they had seen Robert Flaherty's *Man of Aran*, William Wyler's *Wuthering Heights*, and an adaptation of H. G. Wells's *The Island of Dr. Moreau* with the author. They reportedly discussed the Flaherty film at length, not surprising when one considers Joyce's affection for Galway and the Ireland of his Nora. The other films, as the Jolas stated, "should not be quoted as Joyce's decided preferences," but simply as the films that they recall seeing with him (Hutchins, 245). Nino Frank, a journalist acquainted with the author, also mentions films that he attended with Joyce:

> Sometimes we talked about the cinema; James Joyce was interested in the cinema and asked me to take him two or three times.
>
> How can I forget these occasions, painful for me because his poor vision compelled us to sit in the first row? They allowed me to discover his esteem for "grand drama," where, as they say, there is something to sink your teeth into, and for a film of Jean Choux's about Paris, where Harry Baur's well-measured tremolos triumphed. I also remember another time when, with a young admirer who had come from Ireland to see him, we went to a local theater in the outer boulevards: they were showing some western or other inspired by Fenimore Cooper, and it seems to me someone had assured Joyce that he would find in it some plays on words to please him. Such was not the case. (Potts, 99)

No matter what movies Joyce saw, a number of film allusions and cinematic references find their way into *Finnegans Wake*, at times in curious ways. As he looked for ideas to layer the references in the *Wake*, Joyce consulted the magazine *Boy's Cinema* for material for

Book II, the children's book (Ellmann, 616). The cinema even receives a brief mention in the "Circe" section of *Scribbledehobble*, Joyce's notebook for the *Wake*: "cinema fakes, drown, state of sea, tank, steeplejack, steeple on floor, camera above; jumps 10 feet, 1 foot camera in 6 foot pit" (119).

Joyce was not, however, above using the cinema to satisfy interests other than literary. Lucie Noel, Paul Léon's wife, relates a revealing tale:

> I was his "seeing eye" . . . when he took me to see a film in the Rue de Clichy which had been causing some comment. He had tried to get Paul to go, but my husband said the idea bored him. The movie was Extase, in which Hedy Lamarr ran around the countryside perfectly beautiful and quite nude. There was also a very realistic love scene between horses. The picture was quite erotic and I was quite embarrassed, because I had to explain much of the action to Joyce. . . . At that time his eyesight was really bad, and every few minutes he would ask, "What are they doing now?" I would try to tell him in as general a way as I could, and he would say "I see", obviously amused by my fumbling explanation. But we both thought it was a very fine picture. (19)

In this unconventional manner (and perhaps in other ways–see Chapter VI), the author explored the erotic potential of the movies.

Nor was Joyce above being star-struck by a beautiful actress, even in his later years. Mary Colum tells of an evening in which the Joyces met Marlene Dietrich, whom Nora recognized. The two cultural giants were intrigued by one another:

> The effect was electrical. I had not imagined that such a writer would be of interest to a movie star, but both Miss Dietrich and, more naturally, the novelist with her [Erich Maria Remarque] were excited at the encounter. . . . [T]he conversation was continued for a time. "I saw you," Joyce said to the star, as if he were speaking of some event far back in history, "in *L'Ange bleu*." "Then, monsieur," Miss Dietrich replied, "you saw the best of me."
>
> Joyce was amused by it all. "I thought the years when I was a lion were over," he said, smiling, but with a kind of melancholy. (229)

Undoubtedly, however, his most significant encounters with a *cinéaste* were his meetings with Eisenstein in Paris in 1929. In her biography of the Russian, Marie Seton describes the scene:

> So in Paris Sergei Mikhailovich [Eisenstein] went to the home of James Joyce. Though he had already read and re-read Ulysses, and thought he had grasped its subtle nuances, he found he had only begun to understand the book on an elementary level. Only when Joyce read passages to Sergei Mikhailovich (who had never before felt himself to be sitting at the feet of any living master) did its words and images take on their full significance. . . . Despite his near blindness, Joyce wanted to see those sections of Potemkin and October in which Sergei Mikhailovich had tried to reveal the inner core of man and, thus, convey reality to the spectator. (149)

In his autobiography, *Immoral Memories*, Eisenstein expresses the relationship between the two artists as more equal, although his respect for Joyce is still evident: "With great sincerity, Joyce asks me to show him my films, since he has become interested in the experiments in the language of cinema that I am carrying out on the screen (just as I am fascinated by his kindred researches in literature)" (214). Joyce, not to be outdone technologically, cranked the gramophone so that Eisenstein could hear his recent recording of "Anna Livia Plurabelle."[3]

In the next decade, the author found himself and his friends in a very different position within the film industry than as fans and spectators: entertaining proposals to bring *Ulysses* to the screen. According to Ellmann, the projects were numerous, if unrealized:

> Warner Bothers wrote to Joyce about the movie rights. . . . He allowed Paul Leon to keep the matter going, talked with Eisenstein about it, and did not discourage Stuart Gilbert from trying his hand at scenarios for *Ulysses* and *Anna Livia Plurabelle*. (654)[4]

Another scenario of *Ulysses* was attempted by the poets Jerry Reisman and Louis Zukofsky, as Ellmann notes. Joyce read "a large part" of this treatment according to a letter of Paul Leon's. While it contained "a quantity of glaring mistakes," on the whole, "it would seem that it appears . . . quite commendable" (Slate, 119).[5]

While some uncertainty remains regarding Joyce's opinion on the feasibility of filming *Ulysses*, he expressed some ideas about it.[6] After Joyce's meeting with Eisenstein, Eugene Jolas reports "that if *Ulysses* were ever made into a film, he [Joyce] thought the only man who could direct it would be either Walter Ruttman [sic] the German or Sergei Eisenstein the Russian" (Seton, 149). Robert Flaherty, whose work Joyce admired, was also mentioned in connection with the possible production, as Eugene and Maria Jolas tell us. Joyce appears to have made informed choices—his selection of directors suggests, respectively, the dominant tendencies of film and imply the cinematic qualities of his work: the objective, mimetic impulse and that of the subjective creation.

Even though Joyce might not accurately be described as "movie crazy," the mechanical art of film certainly played a role in his commercial and artistic life; at various times in his life he turned to it for both inspiration and relaxation. Exploring its role in his work suggests how the medium and subjects of film influenced Joyce and his modernist texts.

II

Although critics have not entirely ignored the relationship between the cinematic medium and Joyce—as a brief survey of the literature will show—many of the investigations have been brief or superficial, while others have been too mechanical and occasionally misguided.

One of the earliest critical links between Joyce and the cinema was forged by Sergei Eisenstein in his 1929 essay "The Cinematographic Principle and the Ideogram." Eisenstein observes the cinema's representation of psychic disproportion, discussed at some length in Chapter IV of this study. Much of the literary criticism that followed took its cues from Eisenstein.

In his 1932 examination, *The Twentieth Century Novel*, Joseph Warren Beach draws an analogy between the high degree of subjectivism in works by Henry James and Joyce to "the close-up and the slow-up, or *ralenti*, in the moving picture," but concerns himself more with the subjectivity than the relationship between the two arts (408). Harry Levin's 1941 book on the Irishman takes up the affinities between the two media. But apart from the brief parallel drawn between Joyce's style and montage, along with a mention of Eisenstein's praise for the author's "effective applications of this technique," Levin does not systematically analyze the cinematic aspects of Joyce's fiction (108).

The connections between movies and Joyce's fiction remain largely unexplored for the next fifteen years, until Robert Humphrey, in his 1955 study, *Stream of Consciousness in the Modern Novel*, discusses a "set of devices for controlling the movement of stream-of-consciousness fiction . . . that may be termed 'cinematic' devices" (49). He explains that "montage and the secondary devices [fade-outs, close-ups and flashbacks] have to do with transcending or modifying arbitrary and conventional time and space barriers" (49–50). Drawing upon Virginia Woolf's *Mrs Dalloway*, Humphrey illustrates the time-montage, that is "the superimposition of images or ideas from one time to those of another," while the "Wandering Rocks" episode of *Ulysses* displays space-montage in which time remains "fixed and . . . the spatial element changes" (50). In this basic fashion he initiates an analytic exploration of montage in the modern novel.

A few years later Mary Parr demonstrates how interdisciplinary work can go awry in her eccentric study, *James Joyce: The Poetry of Conscience*. Parr boldly claims that Leopold Bloom "is modelled on the supreme clown of them all: Charlie Chaplin" (8). With an acceptance of "Chaplin in Bloom," as she subsequently terms this synthetic persona, "Joyce is released from captivity in the academic world to live among those men and women of all ages who seek a life line to the times in which they live" (9). Although Joyce might have lauded this populist goal, the limitation of his character and aesthetic to one film maker, no matter how influential Chaplin and the "Little Tramp" may have been in the world at large, is excessively reductive. In the second part of her study, Parr examines Joyce's employment of "an 'intellectual cinema' technique in *Ulysses*"—that is, she briefly summarizes Eisenstein's theories of montage as delineated in "The Cinematographic Principle and the Ideogram" and swiftly returns to her discovery of the Bloom/Chaplin synthesis (8).

Marshall McLuhan, in his 1964 *Understanding Media*, returns us to the reasonable link of Joyce and the cinema with a brief mention of its connection with stream-of-consciousness:

> We may now consider a further instance of the film's influence in a most conclusive aspect. In modern literature there is probably no more celebrated technique than that of the stream of consciousness or interior monologue. Whether in Proust, Joyce, or Eliot, this form of sequence permits the reader an extraordinary identification with personalities of the utmost range and diversity. The stream of consciousness is really managed by the transfer of film technique to the printed page. (295)

However, it should be added that, like Eisenstein and D. W. Griffith before him, McLuhan credits Dickens with making use of "filmic" techniques, suggesting that cinematic qualities in literature may predate the invention of the cinematograph and its many innovations throughout this century.[7]

The early sixties also brought another exploration of the parallels between cinema and Joyce's fiction. In a chapter of his book, *A New Approach to Joyce: The* Portrait of the Artist *as a Guidebook*, Robert Ryf explores "Joyce's Visual Imagination" hoping to "restore the balance" of Joyce criticism from its emphasis on the aural aspect of Joyce's work (189). As noted below, Ryf refers to Méliès and he also discusses the relation between the work and thought of Eisenstein and Joyce. After thus establishing the connections between the two artists, he proceeds to document Joyce's "approximations of six standard motion picture techniques . . . : montage, superimposition, the overlap dissolve, flashback, controlled perspective or camera angle, and pictorial lighting," demonstrating similar techniques in the two media (177). His observations regarding these techniques in *Dubliners*, *A Portrait of the Artist as a Young Man*, and *Ulysses* demonstrate various visual techniques in Joyce's canon and consider their critical significance, albeit briefly. However, suggesting literary equivalents to the vocabulary of film methods accomplishes little more than showing that the two media share narrative strategies, rather than an exploration of their intertextuality and complementarity that can offer a deeper analysis of both art forms.

As the decade closes, Paul Deane attempts a similar analysis of "Motion Picture Technique in James Joyce's 'The Dead.'" In his article, he claims that "all major film techniques are present" in the story and he relentlessly proves it (231). Swiftly, he illustrates how in "The Dead," with

> its construction in sequences, scenes, and shots, its varing [sic] focal lengths, flashbacks, flashforwards, intercutting, soft focus, dissolves, several angles of vision, cutting and zooms, James Joyce has, whether consciously or unconsciously, used the major methods of the motion picture. (236)

Deane forces film making labels onto the story without even a mention that similar techniques existed in literature before the cinema appeared; his study, much more so than Ryf's, demonstrates how easily the relationship between literature and film can be reduced to a search for mechanical parallels, rather than as a means to illuminate the interpretation of both media.

The waning of the sixties also heralds the arrival of William York Tindall's *A Reader's Guide to* Finnegans Wake. In the introduction to this handbook, Tindall makes brief but evocative mention of the use of cinema in the *Wake*. He claims that the work's structure reveals Joyce's addiction to the movies. Suggesting that montage can be seen in both *A Portrait of the Artist As a Young Man* and *Ulysses*, he notes that "the placing of matters throughout the *Wake* seems a kind of montage by juxtaposition as the puns seem montage by superimposition" (17). He also notes a few of Joyce's cinematic allusions (to *My Man Godfrey*, *Birth of a Nation*, and *Mr. Deeds Goes to Town*), his movie-related puns ("cinemen," "newseryreel," and "the reel world") and his use of Hollywood gossip in the Peaches and Daddy Browning scandal. In this way, Tindall concisely hints at the range and depth of Joyce's use of filmic techniques and references.

In his 1972 survey of twenty-six major twentieth century playwrights and novelists, *The Cinematic Imagination: Writers and the Motion Pictures*, Edward Murray includes a section on Joyce. He provides a brief survey of Joyce's biographical associations with the cinema, as an entrepreneur and a spectator, as a holder of film rights to his works and an artistic colleague of Eisenstein. The majority of the chapter, however, assesses the failures of two Joycean adaptations: Joseph Strick's 1967 version of *Ulysses* and Mary Ellen Bute's 1965 rendering of *Finnegans Wake*. Between these two, he inserts a four-page review of cinematic techniques in *Ulysses*, discussing its "edited" quality, cataloguing instances of its "cuts" and "crosscuts," its "dissolves," its "slow-motion" and "fast-motion effects," its "close-ups" and "flashbacks" and finally praising the montage qualities of "Wandering Rocks," as observed by Humphrey. The comprehensive list-like nature of his study precludes detailed analysis of these similar techniques in the two media.

In the latter half of the seventies, criticism linking modernism and the cinema, which considers Joyce to an extent, becomes more sophisticated and insightful. Alan Spiegel's 1976 study, *Fiction and the Camera Eye: Visual Consciousness in Film and the Modern Novel*, traces "cinematographic" form in the novel back to Flaubert and his literary descendants: Henry James, Joseph Conrad, and Joyce. While James is faithful to the subject's eye, for example, in *What Maisie Knew*, and Conrad creates a "visual field and a manner of apprehension commensurate with a context of mystery, physical adventure and moral enigma" throughout his canon, Spiegel claims Joyce's works have "a characteristic coldness of vision, a kind of spiritual separateness that begins with a passive, affectless eye"

(55–9; 61; 67). He traces the development of the cinematographic form in this way: there is an

> emergence of a cinematographic form from *Madame Bovary* to *Ulysses* in terms of two changes that occur in the depiction of the external world: (1) a change in emphasis from the object seen to the seer seeing (that is a literal depiction of the observed field as it appears in the image of the retina); and (2) a change in the presentation of the field of vision itself, from a continuous, open and unobstructed presentation to one that is discontinuous, fragmented and incarcerated. (82)

While I believe Spiegel is accurate in his relation of the cinematographic form to the subjectivity and fragmentation of modernist texts, I remain unconvinced by his argument regarding the affectless and cold quality of Joyce's work. Spiegel seems not to acknowledge the humanity, pathos, and humor that infuses Joyce's texts and characters. However, this critical study does demonstrate the fruitfulness of this line of inquiry. In the last section, Spiegel proceeds, with mixed success, to outline four characteristics of cinematographic form: 1) the adventitious (or random) detail, 2) the anatomization of objects and beings as they move through time and space, 3) the depthlessness of all objects equalized on a two-dimensional plane and 4) the use of montage—the "editor's or director's arrangement (mounting) of the various photographed perspectives (shots, the images recorded by all the different camera setups) according to a predetermined concept" (163). Yet, he does not spend enough time on one author or one work to consider the critical significance of his newly delineated cinematographic form.

The affinities that some filmmakers share with Joyce are further explored in an article by Ruth Perlmutter simply titled "Joyce and Cinema." Using a melange of critical terms, films and literary texts, the author explains how Joyce, Eisenstein and Jean-Luc Godard attempt to achieve similar ends in their work. Paralleling the cinema "in its fusion of narrative voices and its cosmophanic accumulation of human experience and observation, *Ulysses* captures the sense of direct experience and, at the same time, mocks all human aspiration to represent the 'ineluctable' modalities of the visible and the audible" (489). In a similar vein, Perlmutter reminds us that Eisenstein praised Joyce for his "physiological organization of emotions" and his abolition of "the distinction between subject and object" (*Film Form*, 185; 104). Godard's film, *Two or Three Things I Know*

About Her, also compares with *Ulysses* in its "dual textuality"—the one text yearning "for the myth of totalization" and the other a "palimpsest . . . of formal deconstructions which exposes that error" (499). In this fashion, Perlmutter suggests how Joyce's narrative prefigures the rhetoric of "intellectual cinema."

Skillfully documenting the similarities between the two media and utilizing an extraordinary wealth of cultural and intellectual history regarding the turn of the century, Keith Cohen in his 1979 work, *Film and Fiction: The Dynamics of Exchange*, considers the relationship of the cinema to literature. By quoting Arnold Hauser and commenting upon his observations, Cohen sums up the relationship between the two art forms astutely:

> 'The discontinuity of the plot and the scenic development, the sudden emersion of the thoughts and moods, the relativity and the inconsistency of the time standards are what remind us in the works of Proust and Joyce, Dos Passos and Virginia Woolf of the cuttings, dissolves and interpolations of the film.' . . . The intrinsic nature and specific techniques of the cinema: standardization of mimetic objects, temporal distortions, shifting point of view, and discontinuous continuity were applicable and ultimately transferrable to the novel in very concrete ways. (84; 87)

As with Spiegel's work, the study is valuable (and Cohen's is the superior work in scope and breadth), yet it still does not fully explore the implications of Joyce's affinities with film, nor does it consider how this burgeoning union of art and technology has altered Joyce's work.

With the work of Spiegel, Cohen and Perlmutter, it appeared that studies of Joyce and cinema acheived a new level of sophistication. But the momentum falters with the work of Craig Wallace Barrow. His 1980 study, *Montage in James Joyce's* Ulysses, returns the field to a period of reductive and mechanistic comparisons. While his introduction regarding the literary and cinematic uses of montage is useful, Barrow quickly zeroes in on Raymond Spottiswoode's distinction between primary and simultaneous montage—that is, as Spottiswoode explains in his *A Grammar of the Film: An Analysis of Film Technique*, between the juxtaposition of shots and the interplay of sound and image. Much of the rest of Barrow's study consists of a plot summary with notations inserted to inform the reader whether primary or simultaneous montage is present. The book's occasional insights do not justify such tedium; montage in Joyce is far too rich a topic to squander. It can reveal underlying assumptions about the technique as it is practiced in both media.

In his 1983 study, *The Novel in Motion: An Approach to Modern Fiction*, Richard Pearce incorporates and revises an earlier essay entitled "Experimentation with the Grotesque: Comic Collisions in the Grotesque World of *Ulysses*." In this book, he offers two sections on Joyce, one on "ways of seeing" in *A Portrait of the Artist As a Young Man* and the other on montage in *Ulysses*. In the earlier novel, he suggests, "Joyce develops from traditional to phenomenal to what we might call modernist picturing—where the medium, our most immediate point of contact, directly stimulates the sensation of movement and calls attention to itself in the process." By the fifth chapter of *Portrait*, "the narrative eye moves faster, shifts its position from far to near, changes its angle from wide to narrow, fragments so sharply that details . . . become an independent source of interest, and brings into focus kinetic patterns that are purely pictorial" (23). Moving on to *Ulysses*, Pearce utilizes Eisenstein's view that montage is conflict and analyzes one-third of the episodes in a brisk ten pages. He considers first the collision of Joyce's characters with their mythic and literary counterparts: Bloom and Ulysses, Stephen and Hamlet; an additional collision occurs between the reader and the text, resulting in the former's dislocation. Both collisions clearly create a third term, a term that resonates with meaning, as Eisenstein suggests will happen when a spectator interprets a montage sequence. However, Pearce spends more time documenting these effects than he does exploring their meaning within the novel's themes and techniques.

The articles concerning Joyce and the cinema from the eighties begin again to treat the issues in a more subtle, full and informed manner. William V. Costanzo's "Joyce and Eisenstein: Literary Reflections on the Reel World" shows how fertile such investigation can be. Like Tindall, he argues that language in *Finnegans Wake* works according to the principles of montage. When presented with the portmanteau words of the *Wake*, the reader sees how words and phonemes mesh to create various meanings, just as the multiple elements of a film montage do:

> When Joyce calls his book a "meanderthalltale" (19.25), he is yoking single words with simple denotation into a new expression, something richer, more complex, more volatile. . . . [T]he combination of neanderthal, meander, and me and the tall tale challenges

the mind to make connections, to synthesize the seemingly familiar into concepts that are yet to be explored. (179)

Thus, Costanzo intriguingly suggests that Joyce has "refashioned the pun in the image of montage" (178). As I discuss in Chapter Four, the word-montage begins much earlier than *Finnegans Wake*.

In a well-researched and skillfully argued article from 1985, "Eisensteinian Montage and Joyce's Ulysses: The Analogy Reconsidered," R. Barton Palmer questions the aptness of the analogy between the montage of Eisenstein and the work of Joyce. He suggests that

> within the heterogeneous context of Ulysses the montage of exterior and interior images is essentially a conservative technique, one which, like Eisensteinian montage itself, remains within the representational problematic of classic realism. What is interesting about the novel, however, is that it also manifests techniques which resemble cinematic montage and whose effect is to overthrow the premises of the realist tradition. (79)

He maintains that Joyce is in fact more radical in his use of montage than Eisenstein ever was. As he describes his test case, "Oxen of the Sun":

> Joyce's procedure, in short, involves the montage-like double process of decomposition/reconstruction. While the narrative signifieds of . . . [the episode], i.e. the events of the birth themselves, the story inferrable [sic] from the separate discourses, constitute an undisrupted whole, the signifiers belong to discrete sets. (82)

Making his departure from an evaluation of Eisensteinian montage, Palmer regards *Ulysses* as a critique of naturalism and demonstrates its metafictional aspects, providing another model of how film theory can be useful to the literary critic.

Deborah Martin Gonzales also challenges the importance of the connection between Joyce and the cinema in her 1986 dissertation "'Drauma' and 'Newseryreel': Joyce's Dramatic Aesthetic in Adaptation." Based on an examination of the numerous stage and screen adaptations of the canon, her study "explores the cinematographic versus theatrical characteristics of Joyce's novels by examining his techniques in light of the distinguishing characteristics of the two genres." She points to "his reliance on dialogue over description, and thus the word over the image, and his panoramic rather than close-up vision," concluding that Joyce's fiction has more in common with the theater than with the cinema. Since her argument relies heavily upon the adaptations to assess qualities of Joyce's work, I believe her to be evaluating the work of the adaptors rather than that of the author; Gonzales, however, maintains that "the portions of an adaptation which work well or badly do so partly because of the original," and since most of the adaptations "lift whole sections of the novels virtually unchanged," they can serve as "gauges of the theatrical or cinematic characteristics of their originals." (See *DAI, 47,* 2594A.)

In the latter half of the eighties, two articles demonstrate that Joyce's debt to the cinema may be greater than Gonzales acknowledges and more specific than most previous commentators had thought. Susan Bazargan offers an interpretation of "The Headings of 'Aeolus': A Cinematographic View," likening them to the explanatory titles of silent pictures. In addition to identifying some pornographic mutoscopes that Bloom mentions in "Nausicaa," Austin Briggs in "'Roll Away the Reel World, the Reel World': 'Circe' and Cinema" describes the parallels between the techniques of Joyce's episode and the trick films of Méliès and the early film criticism of Vachel Lindsay.

As these works suggest, the possible affinities between Joyce and cinema are numerous but thus far have focused primarily on filmic devices within Joyce's texts. What I intend to do is to extend further the work of such critics and attempt to interpret Joyce's works by the light of the cinematograph and its theory, considering both how this nascent art may have offered Joyce new techniques, as well as showing how it also provides us more ways to explicate his fiction.

NOTES

[1] See Chapter VI: "A Look Between" for a fuller exploration of this dynamic as it occurs in "Nausicaa."

[2] Robert Ryf tantalizes one when he points out that during Joyce's student days in Paris he stayed in a hotel a scant two miles from the theatre in which Georges Méliès's films were shown. Perhaps Joyce discovered the potentials of the film medium early on from this innovator. See Robert Ryf, *A New Approach to Joyce: the* Portrait of the Artist *as a Guidebook,* 174.

[3] For more biographical information on the connections and meeting between Joyce and Eisenstein, primarily from the Russian's perspective and materials related to him see Gösta Werner's "James Joyce and Sergej Eisenstein." (See works cited.)

⁴Another director, whose name is lost to memory, also communicated with Joyce or his willing assistants, Stuart Gilbert and Paul Léon: "Between 1934 and 1935 they were in touch with a Hungarian director, whose name Stuart Gilbert has forgotten." See Hutchins, *James Joyce's World*, 245.

⁵For a wealth of information regarding the Reisman-Zukofsky screenplay see Joseph Evans Slate's article in the list of works cited.

⁶In a letter of 1932 to Ralph Pinker, Paul Léon states that "Mr Joyce . . . tells me that he is in principle opposed to the filming of Ulysses," regarding it "irrealisable." Given the legal tone of this missive and the fact that it seems clearly designed to prevent premature "press news . . . about the forthcoming filming of Ulysses" (and ultimately to thwart piracy of the film rights), it seems imprudent to take these as Joyce's artistic opinions about adapting the novel to the screen. (See *Letters*, 3: 263).

⁷Although these techniques may have their origins in the increasing mechanization brought by the Industrial Revolution, their more radical and disconcerting use appear in Modernist texts. (See the discussion of Hugh Kenner's *The Mechanic Muse* in Chapter Two.)

CHAPTER TWO
The New Fashionable Kinematographic Vein

> Indeed, there are moments, rare, it is true, but still to be observed from time to time, when nature becomes absolutely modern.
>
> —Oscar Wilde, "The Decay of Lying"

While Joyce was preparing for and painstakingly crafting the fiction that would transform literature, the society in which he lived underwent a transformation itself; the introduction of new machines such as telephones, phonographs, subways, and typewriters revolutionized early twentieth century urban life. With this revolution arose a general change in perception: the burgeoning modernist sensibility. Characterized in part by fragmentation and streams-of-consciousness, this new perception can be linked to the increased speed of communication and production and the new space-time relationships wrought by these technological innovations. This new modernist aesthetic appears in both literature and cinema and can be analyzed using discussions by Hugh Kenner, Walter Benjamin and Arnold Hauser.

In his short book on modernism and technology, *The Mechanic Muse*, Hugh Kenner entreats us to study how literature relates to the environment in which it was conceived, that is, its social context. The literature of the modern era represents "new ways of writing, then for new orders of experience; urban experience; Modernism is distinctively urban." While Kenner tacitly acknowledges the argument of T. S. Eliot's essay, "Tradition and the Individual Talent," he qualifies it with an important observation: "Like all writing [modernism] does modify earlier writing, partly because in continuity with the past lay the principles by which it could be understood at all. But like all live writing it ingests what's around it." This dual perspective recognizes the value of previous critical source studies, while expanding the field of inquiry:

> How Eliot's verse derives from high Victorian verse is a topic by now well canvassed; or what Joyce owed to Homer and Sterne, Pound to Cavalcanti and even Bliss Carman, Beckett to Synge and Yeats and Arnold Geulincx. It seems time to sketch what they drew from the world around them, not excluding the world-around-them's most salient feature, intelligence questing after what can be achieved by a patterned moving of elements in space: the mats of a linotype, the words of a poem. (14–15)

In his study, Kenner examines the relationship between modernist authors and various technologies. He considers Eliot's poetry in connection with the mechanisms of the alarm clock, the subway and the telephone, all in a crowded urban setting. The machine in general, that is "any economical self-activating system for organizing resources," be it of steel or words, dominates the aesthetic of Pound. With Joyce's fiction, Kenner observes the impact of typesetting: "no writer was ever so observant of the way our lives have come to be governed by marks on paper" (72). In his essay on Beckett, he notes how the language of the machine becomes the novel—Kenner translates a passage of *Watt* into the computer language Pascal and suggests that Beckett already writes "in a proto-computer language" (96).

As Kenner suggests, "technology alters our sense of what the mind does, what are its domains, how characterized and bounded," and the technology of the cinema transforms Joyce's conception of the novel as surely as the various technical innovations affect his work and those of other modernists (109). Certainly, as Walter Benjamin suggests in "The Work of Art in the Age of Mechanical Reproduction": "the manner in which human sense perception is organized, the medium in which it is accomplished, is determined not only by nature but by historical [including technological] circumstances as well" (222). In the cinema's infancy Joyce clearly foresaw its potential and understood its effect on perception, even before the more sophisticated filmic techniques of the teens and twenties were developed. As Ellmann notes, Joyce was always prescient: even the 1982 edition of the biography retains that reverential first sentence, "we are still learning to be James Joyce's contemporaries, to understand our interpreter" (3). If we can analyze the work of Beckett and Eliot more aptly by considering their art's relationship to the telephone and the computer, respectively, then examining the affinities that Joyce's work shares with the cinema may yield similar results. What Kenner recognizes as the most important aspect of the modernists' environment, that "intelligence questing after what can be achieved by a patterned moving of elements in space," can, of course, be achieved forcefully through film. While Kenner omits discussion of the cinema from his study, it seems clear that such a critical study ought to be undertaken, especially in light of Joyce's own connections with the movies.

In his epilogue to *The Mechanic Muse*, Kenner characterizes the modernist period in this fashion:

> Founded on faith in the possibility of insight—the Joycean epiphany, the Poundian image that can flash in an instant of time; on faith, too, that technology need not consign the arts to irrelevance, the Modernist enterprise evolved its verbal technologies, its poem- and novel-machines of intricate interacting discrete pieces. The technology on which it drew for tacit analogies is largely obsolescent now. (110)

But the most important surviving technology may well be the cinema. Joyce availed himself of the affinities of the two media so that one can now use the theory of the cinema to interpret his fictions. As western culture evolves further into what we might call the pixeled universe of the video display terminal, of digitized sound and image, the cinema remains with us as a vestige of the modernist technologies.[1]

Although he never explicitly refers to film, Kenner suggests in his choice of descriptive metaphor the depths to which modernism and the cinema interconnect: "compared to progress on foot or even by hansom these shifts of location [i.e., the movements of characters through the city in *Ulysses*] can seem instantaneous, an effect imitated by *quick cuts* between Joyce's episodes" (11, emphasis added). The mobility and the "discrete packets of experience" created by the modern city and its technology are most readily described in terms of film editing. Although Kenner claims that "newsreel quick-cutting helped prompt *The Waste Land*," his subsequent comment on *Ulysses* indicates that such a technique is no less present in the Dublin of Joyce's imagination (9).

Film, not surprisingly, certainly accords with the aesthetics of fragmentation so frequently associated with modernism. Benjamin develops an extended metaphor between the perspectives of the painter and the camera man, comparing them to magus and surgical doctor:

> How does the cameraman compare with the painter? . . . the magician heals a sick person by the laying on of hands; the surgeon cuts into the patient's body. . . .
>
> Magician and surgeon compare to painter and cameraman. The painter maintains in his work a natural distance from reality, the cameraman penetrates deeply into its web. There is a tremendous difference between the pictures they obtain. That of the painter is a total one, that of the cameraman consists of multiple fragments which are assembled under a new law. Thus, for contemporary man the representation of reality by the film is incomparably more significant than that of the painter, since it offers, precisely because of the thoroughgoing permeation of reality with mechanical equipment, an aspect of reality which is free of all equipment. (233–34)

But the cinema does not represent solely an appropriate means for a mimesis of exterior reality or the technique of fragmentation. It also draws upon and reinforces the modernist view of the human psyche. According to Benjamin, dadaism and the cinema are linked: "Dadaism attempted to create by pictorial—and literary—means the effects which the public today seeks in the film" (237). The art produced by the dadaists

> promoted a demand for the film, the distracting element of which is also primarily tactile, being based on changes of place and focus which periodically assail the spectator. . . . No sooner has his eye grasped a scene than it is already changed. It cannot be arrested. . . . The spectator's process of association in view of these images is indeed interrupted by their constant, sudden change. This constitutes the shock effect of the film, which, like all shocks, should be cushioned by heightened presence of mind. (238)

These descriptions of both dada and the movies, those "changes of place and focus which periodically assail the spectator" whose "process of association in view of these images is indeed interrupted by their constant, sudden change," suggest Joyce's style throughout much of *Ulysses* and aptly describe the stream-of-consciousness technique. It may also explain some of the contemporary critical reaction to the novel: an unsigned review of April 8, 1922, from the *Evening News* describes the style of *Ulysses* as being "in the new fashionable kinematographic vein, very jerky and elliptical," while Shane Leslie laments in the *Quarterly Review* of October of the same year that "the confusion of the book is so great that there is no circumventing its clumsiness and unwinding its deliberate bamboozlement of the reader. With an occasional lucid bait the attention is gripped, and then the expectant eye is lost in incoherent fantasies" (Deming, 194, 210). Such comments by contemporary reviewers affirm Kenner's contentions that "[i]n that age of transparent technology, literature evolved parallel technologies of its own, 'difficult,' 'obscure,' before readers had formed habits of adequate patience, adequate attention" (10). Joyce's readers had yet to understand the author's instructions on how to read his works, embedded as they are within the text, nor were they ready to accept the interaction between the novel and the cinema that an anonymous newspaper reviewer recognizes, albeit with disdain.

Prepared or not, however, readers of Joyce's fiction frequently confront techniques that resemble those of the cinema. In discussing "Grace," Kenner notes the presence of many religious terms in a passage relating to Tom Kernan's appearance—in fact, the conflation of spiritual and social respectability is "what the story . . . has to say about Dublin religion." Kenner claims that such

> clustering of vocabularies into overlapping fields is something Joyce took great pains with. It comports with the fact that all printed words, unlike words on living tongues are absolutely neutral. We can't tell what they mean till we can size up their neighbors. (78)

While few, if any, printed words are entirely neutral, the combination of words that such a technique employs parallels that of montage. One needs only consider Lev Kuleshov's famous editing experiment to recognize the similarities. The Russian film maker created three versions of a film, each one intercutting the same image of an actor's face with shots of a bowl of soup, a child playing, and a dead woman; each of the trio of short films elicited praise from its audiences for the actor's skillful portrayal of hunger, joy and sorrow, respectively.

Yet the similarities between Joyce's novels and the cinema involve much more than the use of montage. A fundamental change regarding the nature and perception of time occurs with the nearly concurrent advent of the technology of film, the theory of relativity and the philosophy of Henri Bergson. With "the Bergsonian concept of time," Arnold Hauser observes in *The Social History of Art*,

> the accent is now on the simultaneity of the contents of consciousness, the immanence of the past in the present, the constant flowing together of the different periods of time, the amorphous fluidity of inner experience, the boundlessness of the stream of time by which the soul is borne along, the relativity of space and time, that is to say, the impossibility of differentiating and defining the media in which the mind moves. . . . The new concept of time . . . dates from the same period as Bergson's philosophy of time. . . . [O]ne has the feeling that the time categories of modern art altogether must have arisen from the spirit of cinematic form. (939–40)

From this perspective, Joyce's work and the stream-of-consciousness technique can be said to epitomize what Hauser has characterized as the "film age," as he entitles this chapter of his history. It is a *Zeitgeist* in which time and space are no longer separate qualities; with film and its perceptual set, "the boundaries of space and time are fluid—space has a quasi-temporal, time, to some extent, a spatial character" (940).

In a lengthy discussion, Hauser delineates what he regards as the essential elements created for fiction by this mutability of time and space, characteristics that Robert Humphrey would later discuss:

> [A]s if space and time in the film were interchangeable, the temporal relationships acquire an almost spatial character, just as space acquires a topical interest and takes on temporal characteristics, in other words, a certain element of freedom is introduced into the succession of their moments. In the temporal medium of a film we move in a way that is otherwise peculiar to space, completely free to choose our direction, proceeding from one phase of time into another, just as one goes from one room to another, disconnecting the individual stages in the development of events and grouping them, generally speaking, according to the principles of spatial order. In brief, time here loses, on the one hand, its uninterrupted continuity, on the other its irreversible direction. (941)

The applicability of these notions for the novel will be apparent to any reader of *Ulysses*: the temporality of "Wandering Rocks" is given a spatial character, while the freedom of choice in direction— "from one of time into another"—occurs in all the various streams-of-consciousness which we are invited to enter. For instance, in the first paragraphs of "Proteus," by way of Stephen's learned philosophical and literary allusions, we glide between Aristotle, Jakob Boehme, Bishop Berkeley, and Gotthold Lessing, and read references, both obvious and obscure, to Dante, Dr. Johnson, William Blake, an unidentified Scotsman and two nineteenth century French artists, Madeleine Lemaire, a watercolorist, and Phillipe-Joseph Henri Lemaire, a sculptor. (See Gifford, 44–46.)

Within the nascent medium of film and its conceptions, Hauser notes that time also

> can be brought to a standstill: in close-ups; reversed: in flashbacks; repeated: in recollections; and skipped across: in visions of the future. Concurrent simultaneous events can be shown successively, and temporally distinct events simultaneously—by double-exposure and alternation; the earlier can appear later, the later before its time. This cinematic conception of time has a thoroughly subjective and apparently irregular character. (941)

Ulysses contains numerous examples of all these devices, among them: the close-up occurs with Stephen's shaving-bowl in "Telemachus"; the reversal of film is evidenced in "Proteus" in a ghoulish way as a man is pieced back together—"Shoot him to bloody bits with a bang shotgun, bits man splattered walls all brass buttons. Bits all khrrrrklak in place clackback" (3.187–189); the mental image and presence of Rudy along with refrains from *Sweets of Sin* are repeated as recollections; "the earlier does appear later" in the cards with which Molly prophesies her future in "Calypso," an incident that we remain largely ignorant of until her soliloquy[2]; "the later can be found before its time" in the prelude of the fugue of the "Sirens."

Hauser also posits a relationship between the qualities given to space and time and the stream-of-consciousness technique:

> Joyce fights for the same inwardness, the same directness of experience, when he, like Proust, breaks up and merges well-articulated, chronologically organized time. In his work, too, it is the interchangeability of the contents of consciousness which triumphs over the chronological arrangement of the experiences . . . But he pushes the spatialization of time . . . and shows the inner happenings not only in longitudinal but also in cross–sections. The images, ideas, brainwaves and memories stand side by side with sudden and absolute abruptness; hardly any consideration is paid

to their origins, all the emphasis is on their contiguity, their simultaneity. (945–46)

Any number of passages from *Ulysses* could illustrate such a spatialization, but perhaps none so well as the famous "eight sentences" of "Penelope," as Joyce described the episode's format to Budgen (*Letters*, I, 170). In the soliloquy, contiguity is rarely interrupted by a full stop and a sense of simultaneity is heightened by the ambiguity of many of the pronoun references.

This new apperception of time also bears a relation to the Joycean portrayal of situation. The depiction of time in *Ulysses* can perhaps be best represented by this statement of Hauser:

> It is the simultaneous nearness and remoteness of things—their nearness to one another in time and their distance from one another in space—that constitutes that spatio-temporal element, that two-dimensionality of time, which is the real medium of the film and the basic category of its world-picture. (943)

This "simultaneous nearness and remoteness" is, of course, illustrated both by the temporo-spatial grid of "Wandering Rocks" mentioned above, as well as by the synchronous openings of "Telemachus" and "Calypso," which are spatially separated by both Dublin's urban geography and the pages of the novel.

The conception of time presented in *Finnegans Wake* may be seen in another of Hauser's observations regarding the nature of film:

> As a result of the discontinuity of time, the retrospective development of the plot is combined with the progressive in complete freedom, with no kind of chronological tie, and through the repeated twists and turns in the time-continuum, mobility . . . is pushed to the uttermost limits. (942–43)

While Hauser may not have realized that those limits could be pushed to the extent they are in Joyce's last epic, such a time-continuum describes aptly the many temporal and historical twists and turns that can be found on any page—indeed, in most sentences and words—of the *Wake*.

In his discussion of the space-time continuum, Hauser also refers to the "famous finish of the early, already classical Griffith films, in which the upshot of an exciting plot is made to depend on whether a train or a car, the intriguer or the 'king's messenger on horseback' reaches the goal first" (943). However, perhaps more relevant to a discussion of *Finnegans Wake* is Griffith's own epic, *Intolerance*, which, like Joyce's final work, presents stories that are spatially and temporally distinct, but thematically linked by the recurrence of bigotry and prejudice alluded to in Griffith's title, rather than by the "taling" of the family romance and human history which constitutes the *Wake* (213.12).

This new concept of time also has an effect on character in Joyce's novels. In both *Ulysses* and the *Wake*, Bloom and HCE, Molly and ALP, respectively, serve as two versions of everyman and everywoman. Hauser discusses the relationship of time to these two perceptions of character in this way:

> The fascination of 'simultaneity,' the discovery that, on the one hand, the same man experiences so many different, unconnected and irreconcilable things in one and the same moment, and that, on the other, different men in different places often experience the same things, that the same things are happening at the same time in places completely isolated from each other, this universalism, of which modern technics have made contemporary man conscious, is perhaps the real source of the new conception of time and of the whole abruptness with which modern art describes life. (944)

The stream-of-consciousness technique, the thoughts of Bloom and Molly show how "many different, unconnected and irreconcilable things" occur within our experience at every moment. They represent all humans in the approach of their consciousness to the reality swirling about them; while each individual may have a distinct mental vernacular, all of us can identify with the process of their thoughts. HCE and ALP, on the other hand, represent the concept of universalism with a vengeance. Not only does Joyce portray different people in distinct places sharing similar experiences, he also depicts those in different times and cultures as much the same. This representation of universalism allows Joyce to create HCE as a composite character, with avatars as historically diverse as Finn MacCool, Noah, King Arthur, Oscar Wilde, the Duke of Wellington and Osiris. Such recurring themes in universal history permit ALP to be assigned a similar range of roles, from Mrs. Finnegan, Eve and Guinevere, to Kitty O'Shea, Hera, and Cordelia. (See Adaline Glasheen's chart "Who Is Who When Everybody Is Somebody Else," lxxii–lxxxiv.)

Yet the film aesthetic extends beyond the portrayal of the individual character to the presentation of different realities. As developed by the Russians, Hauser notes,

> the revolutionary quality of . . . montage technique . . . was no longer the phenomena of a homogeneous world of objects, but of quite heterogeneous elements of reality, . . . brought face to face. Thus Eisenstein showed the following sequence in The Battleship Potemkin: men working desperately, engine room of the cruiser; busy hands, revolving wheels; faces distorted with exertion, maximum pressure of the manometer; a chest soaked with perspiration, a glowing boiler; an arm, a wheel; a wheel, an arm; machine, man; machine, man; machine, man. Two utterly different realities, a spiritual and a material, were joined . . . and identified . . . , the one proceeding from the other. But such a . . . trespassing presupposed a philosophy which denies the autonomy of the individual spheres of life, as surrealism does, and as historical materialism has done from the very beginning. (953–54)

Joyce's unifying factor, however, is an aesthetic one, neither bound by the tenets of historical materialism, nor adhering to the manifestoes of surrealism. One finds analogies similar to those of Eisenstein's *Potemkin* within *Ulysses* throughout many episodes. The lunching masses and their animalistic descriptions and the mating flies linked to the Blooms' domestic situation in "Lestrygonians" (8.650–90, 917–18), and the milk woman in "Telemachus," with her "old shrunken paps" as a vision of Ireland may all be seen in this light (1.398).

Hauser characterizes this film aesthetic with a phrase reminiscent of the early Stephen Daedalus's philosophical musings: "things take the place of ideas; things which expose the ideological character of ideas" (953–54). Such a statement recalls the famous definition of epiphany from *Stephen Hero*:

> By an epiphany he meant a sudden spiritual manifestation, whether in the vulgarity of speech or of gesture or in a memorable phase of the mind itself. He believed that it was for the man of letters to record these epiphanies with extreme care, seeing that they themselves are the most delicate and evanescent of moments. (211)

This conception of epiphany, which can encompass even the evanescent moments of inanimate objects like the clock of the Ballast Office, allows things to take the place of ideas. It permits objects to expose and express the ideological character of concepts, or as Bloom puts it, "[e]verything speaks in its own way" (7.177). Even the thoughts of Howth Hill are expressed in "Nausicaa": "Howth settled for slumber, tired of long days, of yumyum rhododendrons (he was old) and felt gladly the night breeze lift, ruffle his fell of ferns. He lay but opened a red eye unsleeping, deep and slowly breathing, slumberous but awake" (13.1176–80). In this way both the techniques of film and novel, as well as their aesthetics, coincide.

Ultimately, of course, the artistic style of an age, its aesthetic theories and the acts of perception cannot be separated. The world of the modernists is influenced by the period's arts, philosophies and technologies. As Walter Benjamin states in his essay on mechanical reproduction, "the characteristics of the film lie not only in the manner in which man presents himself to mechanical equipment but also in the manner in which, by means of this apparatus, man can represent his environment" (235). It is this relationship to art that gives us, among other features, a new perception of time and space, the aesthetic of fragmentation and the stream-of-consciousness technique in the works of the modernists. Or, as Oscar Wilde has Vivian argue in "The Decay of Lying," this relation creates such qualities:

> Where, if not from the Impressionists, do we get those wonderful brown fogs that come creeping down our streets, blurring the gaslamps and changing the houses into monstrous shadows? To whom, if not to them and their master, do we owe the lovely silver mists that brood over our river, and turn to faint forms of fading grace curved bridge and swaying barge? The extraordinary change that has taken place in the climate of London during the last ten years is due entirely to this particular school of Art. (Wilde, 232)

Is there any wonder then that the invention of the cinematograph changed Joyce's perception of the modern world and his idea of what modernist art ought to do? As Vivian continues to assert: "Nature is no great mother who has borne us. She is our creation. It is in our brain that she quickens to life. Things are because we see them, and what we see, and how we see it, depends on the Arts that have influenced us" (232–33).

NOTES

[1] The Internet's effect on the production and marketing of film has yet to be standardized, nor fully realized.

[2] Bloom makes a brief reference to the cards in "Lotus-Eaters": "Blackened court cards laid along her thighs by sevens" (5.155).

CHAPTER THREE
Bioscope
Portraits of Reality

—The question is, I said, is literature to be fact or is it to be an art?

—It should be life, Joyce replied, and one of the things I could never get accustomed to was the difference between life and literature.

—Arthur Power, Conversations with James Joyce

That which enthralls us all—the commonplace.

—Goethe

Among the important elements common to both literature and cinema is that each medium frequently purports to create a picture of life, to represent external reality. Yet there persists a tension between artifice and realism in the mimetic creations. André Bazin eloquently describes the nature of this tension: "The real like the imaginary in art is the concern of the artist alone. The flesh and blood of reality are no easier to capture than are the gratuitous flights of the imagination.... Realism in art can only be achieved in one way—through artifice" (2: 25–26).

Cinematic art usually combines the mimetic and the imagined, in varying proportions. In an article on these dual filmic traditions in *Citizen Kane*, David Bordwell begins by delineating "the two founts of cinema—the fantasy of Méliès and the reportage of Lumière." He summarizes these tendencies in this fashion: "Since Lumière, motion pictures have been attracted to *the detailed reproduction of external reality*.... But running parallel to this documentary trend is *a sub-*

jectivity that uses film to transform reality to suit the creator's imagination" (39, emphasis added). Truly, however, narrative film (and, from a critical perspective, documentary cinema as well) unites these traditions, as Bordwell suggests; within his *magnum opus*, Welles explores and exploits both aspects to create and investigate the world and biography of the enigma, the mystery who is Charles Foster Kane. The film, as Bordwell writes,

> explores the nature of consciousness chiefly by presenting various points of view on a shifting, multiplaned world. We enter Kane's consciousness as he dies, before we have even met him; he is less a character than a stylized image. Immediately, we view him as a public figure—fascinating but remote. Next we scrutinize him as a man, seen through the eyes of his wife and his associates, as a reporter traces his life story. Finally, these various perspectives are capped by a detached, omniscient one. In all, Kane emerges as a man pathetic, grand, contradictory, ultimately enigmatic. The film expresses an ambiguous reality through formal devices that stress both the objectivity of fact and the subjectivity of point of view. (39)

This combination, of course, echoes the development of the English novel, as it moves from narrative documents (the Newgate Calendar) to fiction that purports to be a document (*The Fortunes . . . of Moll Flanders . . . Written from her own Memorandums*) to later fiction with all of the subjective devices it subsequently develops (for example, the narrator of *The Good Soldier* or the "dual consciousness" of Henry James's work).

The audience comes to believe in the reality of both the photographed object and the novel's scenes: whereas viewers tend to grant the photograph's "faithfulness" immediately, the novel's "accuracy" represents readers' gradual acceptance and approval of conventions acknowledged as realistic, an assent to a code. Although he had frequently faced rejection and braved vitriol for his innovations, Joyce predicted that such a pact would eventually develop between the modern author and his audience: "in time people will accept . . . so-called modern distortion and regard it as the truth" (Power, 74). As Ian Watt suggests, "the narrative method whereby the novel embodies . . . [a] circumstantial view of life may be called its formal realism"; it is

> the narrative embodiment of . . . the premise, or primary convention, that the novel is a full and authentic report of human experience. . . .

> Formal realism is, of course, like the rules of evidence, only a convention; and there is no reason why the report on human life which is presented by it should be in fact any truer than those presented through the very different conventions of other literary genres. (32)

The acknowledgment of a reality within the novel allows Joyce to place the pseudo-realistic alongside the real in *Ulysses*. Since we credit the existence of Leopold Bloom, ad canvasser, we understandably might, along with Jack Power in "Cyclops," think the novel's protagonist a relative of—or perhaps confuse him with—Marcus J. Bloom, the oral surgeon whose "dental windows" make a cameo appearance in "Wandering Rocks," on 2 Clare Street (see Gifford or *Thom's Dublin Post Office Directory* for 1904; *Ulysses*, 10.1115, 12.1638–40). Joyce has taken extraordinary care to create as realistic a context as possible in *Ulysses*: for example, the intricate mapping and precise timing of the routes of so many Dubliners in "Wandering Rocks" initially may encourage readers to believe such putative "facts" as Bloom's budget, presented in "Ithaca," which omits certain items. Who would not believe a writer who, as Hugh Kenner has written "can get down a cat's word accurately—'Mrkrgnao'—or make us *see* a mere tea-kettle on the fire— 'It sat there, dull and squat, its spout stuck out'"? (46)

But neither pictorial nor literary realism can claim absolute verisimilitude: Susan Sontag's observations from *On Photography* bear as much, if not more, relevance to literature as they do to their original subject. She explains the relationship between object and representation in this way: "despite the presumption of veracity that gives all photographs authority, interest, seductiveness, the work that photographers do is no generic exception to the usually shady commerce between art and truth" (6). This observation may be applied to many individuals important in connection with this study: to Joyce in his aesthetic statements and in his fiction, to two potential adaptors of *Ulysses* to film (the documentary filmmakers, Robert Flaherty and Walther Ruttmann), and to the essays of André Bazin, whose appreciation of neorealist cinema bears relevance to the realistic elements of Joyce's work.

In an early essay entitled "Drama and Life," Joyce defines one aspect of his artistic goals, finding art and beauty in the mundane:

> [O]ut of the dreary sameness of existence, a measure of dramatic life may be drawn. Even the most-commonplace . . . may play a

part in a great drama. . . . Life we must accept *as we see it before our eyes*, men and women as we meet them in the real world. (45, emphasis added)

This insistent emphasis of Joyce is rooted in the belief that sublunary reality is the appropriate source of drama. Such a perspective links Joyce to both the documentary film maker and the aesthetic of the Italian neorealists discussed below. Thus, for instance, the dilemma of Bob Doran in "The Boarding House," Mr. Duffy's tepid affair with Mrs. Sinico from "A Painful Case," Bloom's paternal protectiveness toward Stephen and his defense of love to the Dubliners in the pub are all the stuff of terrene drama. Later in life, Joyce suggested in more specific terms how commonplace the subjects of art may be: "most lives are made up like the modern painter's themes, of jugs, and pots and plates, back streets and blowsy living rooms inhabited by blowsy women, and of a thousand daily sordid incidents which seep into our minds no matter how we strive to keep them out. These are the furniture of our life" (Power, 75). Furthermore, the *littérateur* possesses a remarkable power of transformation over such actions and objects, according to Joyce:

Don't you think . . . there is a certain resemblance between the mystery of the Mass and what I am trying to do? . . . trying in my poems to give people some kind of intellectual pleasure or spiritual enjoyment by converting the bread of everyday life into something that has a permanent artistic life of its own . . . for their mental, moral, and spiritual uplift. (Stanislaus Joyce, 103–04)

That Joyce achieved a permanent artistic life for his works (and a nearly cult-like status for himself) is attested to by the presence of the Joyce "industry," from its critical tradition to its celebrations of Bloomsday and Joyce's birthday with conferences, parties and banquets to iconography, such as the deck of playing cards with *Ulysses*-inspired images. But more importantly, each of the four major works accomplishes preeminently (but not exclusively) a portion of the stated goal—in the order of their publication: morally, spiritually, mentally uplifting and artistically enduring. In *Dubliners*, written so as to exude the city's "special odour of corruption," Joyce explicitly intended "to write a chapter of the moral history of my country" (*Letters*, 2: 123; 2: 134). *A Portrait of the Artist as a Young Man* combines the conventions of the *bildungsroman* with those of the spiritual biography to document the forging of one artistic conscience, to illustrate the development of a high priest of art. In addition to its various intellectual delights, *Ulysses* has rendered a permanent artistic life to that day when Nora Barnacle first walked out with the author. Perhaps more significantly, the novel transfigures an ordinary man, whose life is fraught with quotidian problems, into a modern Odysseus. In *Finnegans Wake*, of course, one has the systematic and chaotic conversion of the bread of the mundane (in almost every era and location) into an everlasting artistic existence. All these works demonstrate the ways in which Joyce, the Jesuit manqué, secularized the transubstantiation, performing his magic upon the altar of life.

In a manner reminiscent of the early *actualités* of the Lumière brothers—the titles of which explicitly describe their subjects: *The Arrival of a Train at La Ciotat Station*, *Baby's Meal* and *Workers Leaving the Factory* (all from 1895)—Joyce features ordinary scenes from real life in his work. Throughout his narratives, Joyce painstakingly creates numerous mimetic settings: the quays of the Liffey representing "the spectacle of Dublin's commerce" are pictured in "An Encounter" (*Dubliners*, 23), Stephen's thoughtful walks through Dublin in the latter sections of *Portrait* can be accurately charted, both Bloom's escape from the Citizen in "Cyclops" and the cavalcade of Dubliners in "Wandering Rocks" recreate Dublin's urban geography with remarkable precision. This accuracy is evidenced not only by the requests for information found in correspondence to his relatives in Ireland, at first from Stanislaus and later from his aunt, Josephine Murray, but also by the legitimate (though ultimately unrealized) fear of a libel action that *Dubliners* instilled in George Roberts of Maunsel & Company, the second publisher to return the collection after initial acceptance, due to the naming of actual commercial establishments (*Letters*, 2: 313). Joyce's work remains mimetic and realistic without enduring the scientific theories or the "coarse biologism of the naturalists," as Lukács aptly characterizes the author's immediate realist literary predecessors (8). As André Bazin points out, "In France, 'naturalism' goes hand in hand with the multiplication of novels and plays *à thèse*. The originality of Italian neorealism as compared with the chief schools of realism that preceded it . . . lies in never making reality the servant of some *à priori* point of view" (2: 64). Certainly Bazin's observations about Vittorio De Sica and Roberto Rossellini may also be applied to the realist narratives of *Dubliners*, stories in which no social or scientific theses are imposed by the author; instead, conclusions arise contextually from the incidents portrayed.

Joyce's opinions on the drama of life and his corollary penchant for noticing, and later recreating in his work, even the most minute details of an event, suggest that the cinema affected his aesthetic. The recording capability of the camera may, in part, have inspired Joyce to attempt a conception of mimesis within his works: that is, a true copy of the visible world, one of exacting verisimilitude. Yet, defining art succinctly as "the human disposition of sensible or intelligible matter for an aesthetic end" as he assumed the role of aesthetic philosopher in Paris in 1903, Joyce observed in his notebook that photography was not an art:

> Question: Can a photograph be a work of art?
>
> Answer: A photograph is a disposition of sensible matter and may be so disposed for an aesthetic end but it is not a human disposition of sensible matter. Therefore it is not a work of art. (Critical Writings, 145–146)[1]

But the young aesthetician's dismissal of the human element in photography does not hold much sway—one might as well dismiss the human disposition of sensible matter in painted photorealism, regarding brush, palette and hand alike as merely tools. Photography, be it still or moving, can be "a human disposition of sensible matter" for an aesthetic end. As Benedetto Croce suggests, photography can only be artistic if it reveals the presence of a human agent: if the photograph has "in it anything artistic, it will be to the extent that it transmits the intuition of the photographer, his point of view, the pose and grouping which he has striven to attain" (733).

Even in pursuit of the realistic, the camera is not simply objective in its recording; the nature of the "documentary" must be examined carefully. Since the inception of photography, it has been a commonplace notion to regard filmed images as a true representation of reality. "The daguerreotype," wrote Louis Daguerre to entice investors, "is not merely an instrument which serves to draw nature . . . [it] gives her the power to reproduce herself" (Sontag, 188). Likewise, "documentary" films frequently create the appearance of an unmitigated picture of reality. But the apparent sense of objectivity is deceptive and virtually unattainable in any work of art, no matter how realistic the piece seems. Still, the *illusion* of a seamless evocation of a natural universe created by the artist would appeal to Joyce. He could then achieve Flaubert's goal, as recast by Stephen Dedalus: the "artist, *like the God of the creation*, remains within or behind or beyond or above his handiwork, invisible, refined out of existence, indifferent, paring his fingernails" (*Portrait*, 215; emphasis added).[2] Both novelists and documentary filmmakers aspire to this godlike status.

As noted in Chapter One, Robert Flaherty was mentioned as one of the possible directors of the proposed 1930s film version of *Ulysses*. Although universally regarded as a pioneer in documentary film making, his approach to these projects was not always a quest for absolute authenticity; neither the ethics of journalism nor scholarship bound him. The recommendation that Flaherty be involved in the contemplated production implicitly raises many issues about what constitutes a documentary, especially those made by such a pioneering film maker.

Joyce would have praised the artistic impulse behind Flaherty's manipulation of reality within his documentaries, a tendency so much of Joyce's work shares. The word documentary itself, coined by John Grierson in a 1926 review of Flaherty's South Seas film, *Moana*, is derived from *documentaire*, the French word for a travelogue. In later work, Grierson, apologist, champion and philosopher of the documentary film, refines the term, considering it "the creative treatment of actuality" or the "arrangements, rearrangements, and creative shapings of" what he regards as "natural material" (Katz, 345; Grierson, 146). Once the creative aspect is admitted into the formula, as it inevitably must be in the production of a film, the pretense of an unadorned actuality vanishes. But Flaherty and his critics recognized this characteristic throughout his career. Grierson and others accused him of constructing primitivist, neo-Rousseauesque fictions of the noble savage; yet on even more basic levels, distortions occurred. Beginning with the filming of *Nanook*, Flaherty's documentary films were never completely accurate portrayals of the life of his subjects. Nanook learned a new method of capturing seals for the film; the Samoans no longer made their lava-lavas from bark nor did they regularly practice tattooing as shown in two sequences in *Moana*, and the inhabitants of Aran had not hunted a basking shark for generations until they landed one from a curragh for Flaherty's camera. Joyce, as Madame Jolas reports, enjoyed *Man of Aran* and we do not know if he was aware of the ruse or if he was fooled by Flaherty's "realistic" portrayal of a culture, as most audiences undoubtedly were. Although the author argues to Grant Richards against changing any of the "objectionable" details of *Dubliners*, claiming that "he is a very bold man who dares to alter in the presentment, still more to deform, whatever he has seen and heard" and further firmly believes that Richards "will retard the course of civilisation in Ireland by preventing the Irish people from having one good look at themselves in my nicely polished looking-glass," *Dubliners* is not consistently realistic (*Letters*, 2: 134; 1: 64). The figure on top of the harp, for example, described, in the midst of the meticulously mapped routes of Corley and Lenehan of "Two Gallants," as "heedless that her coverings had fallen about her knees, seemed weary alike of the eyes of strangers and of her master's hands," represents the type of metaphor invoked by the author to reflect his view of subjugated Dublin (*Dubliners*, 54). Such metaphors occur occasionally throughout the predominantly realistic stories: other examples include "all the seas of the world" which tumble about Eveline's heart as she is "passive, like a helpless animal" and the houses in the opening paragraph of "Araby," "conscious of decent lives within them" while gazing at one other with their "brown imperturbable faces" (*Dubliners*, 41; 29). These examples suggest that Joyce, as a weaver of texts and a maker of fictions, would endorse Flaherty's defense of the liberties taken in representation: "Sometimes you have to lie. . . . One often has to distort a thing to catch its true spirit" (Calder-Marshall, 97). Just as Flaherty's basking shark sequence established the Aran Islanders as a people who struggled with the sea, Joyce's embellishments to his realism call the reader's attention to the paralysis of the Irish capital. As Joyce told Arthur Power, "all art in a sense is distorted in that it must exaggerate certain aspects to obtain its effect" (74).

The artistic impulse that creates a work based in reality that urges the creator to present a seemingly unmitigated slice of life may also be compared to the drive behind Italian neorealist film, a style championed by André Bazin in many of his essays, particularly "In Defense of Rossellini" and "An Aesthetic of Reality: Cinematic Realism and the Italian School of the Liberation." Bazin's comments on Italian neorealism are telling; many of the terms that he uses may also be fruitfully applied to Joyce's *Dubliners*.

The narratives in both consist of "actual day to day events" and "reconstituted reportage." From the plausible and the mundane, film maker and writer produce art; the theft of a bicycle in Rome or a visit to a closing bazaar in Dublin provides a focus for social drama. Both neorealist films and *Dubliners* "could not unfold in just any social context, historically neutral," thus lending to both "an exceptionally documentary quality" (Bazin, 2: 20). In each, "hundreds of . . . meaningful details multiply the vital links between the scenario and the actuality, situating the event in political and social history, in a given place, at a given time" (Bazin, 2: 50). Which is not to suggest that the narratives hold little appeal for those of other cultures: Ezra Pound, in a review of Eliot's *Prufrock and Other Observations*, notes that the best criticism of *Ulysses* "has come from a Belgian who said, 'All this is as true of my country as of Ireland'" (*Literary Essays*, 420). Furthermore, as Joyce himself told Arthur Power, "for myself, I always write about Dublin, because if I can get to the heart of Dublin, I can get to the heart of all the cities of the world. In the particular is contained the universal" (Magalaner, 19). And in the fictional, one may find a representation that seems true.

In both the filmed and printed narratives, "the necessity inherent in the narrative is biological rather than dramatic. It burgeons and grows with all the verisimilitude of life" (Bazin, 2: 31); such a narrative approach frequently leaves first-time readers of Joyce's stories with the impression that "nothing happens." "An Encounter" chronicles an adventurous young boy's truancy, while "A Little Cloud" sketches an evening out with two old friends: "Little" Chandler and Ignatius Gallaher. That the stories subtly explore bourgeois values and Dublin's mores often occur to a reader only after repeated exposures and patient study; the numerous details of the stories, brimming with significance, enhance the realistic qualities of the narratives.

But the realism of *Dubliners* and neorealist films offers more than a replete verisimilitude: "Neorealism tends to give back to the cinema a sense of the ambiguity of reality." For neorealism, the "fact" is a "unit of cinematic narrative,"

> a fragment of concrete reality in itself multiple and full of ambiguity, whose meaning emerges only after the fact, thanks to other imposed facts between which the mind establishes certain relationships. . . . Each image being on its own just a fragment of reality existing before any meanings, the entire surface of the scene should manifest an equally concrete density. (2:37)

Such fragments from Dubliners include words like "gnomon" and "simony" from "The Sisters," the omitted verse from the song in "Clay," and objects such as the dead priest's yellowing books and the bicycle pump in the garden in "Araby." The significance of these "facts" and fragments of reality is still debated by Joyceans. In *Dubliners* (and throughout *Ulysses*), as in neorealism: "The events are not necessarily signs of something, of a truth of which we are to be convinced, they all carry their own weight, their complete uniqueness, that ambiguity that characterizes any fact" (Bazin, 2:52).

Significantly, Bazin contrasts the Italian films with the French literary realist tradition, comparing Rossellini's film work to Zola's novels:

> The traditional realist artist—Zola, for example—analyzes reality into parts which he then reassembles in a synthesis the final determinant of which is his moral conception of the world, whereas the consciousness of the neorealist director filters reality. Undoubtedly, his consciousness, like that of everyone else, does not admit reality as whole, but the selection that does occur is neither logical nor psychological; it is ontological in that the image of reality it restores to us is still a whole. . . . There is ontological identity between the object and its photographic image. (2: 98)

For *Dubliners* and the realistic portions of *Ulysses* and *Portrait*, this ontological relationship between object and image is ostensibly as consistent as the one of object and photograph. Remember Joyce's assertion to Grant Richards concerning the artist who deforms the reality he presents: Joyce wants his readers to believe in the veracity of the image reflected by his looking-glass, so carefully polished in order to reflect the situation of Dublin without the unabashed distortion of a moral conception, or an *à priori* significance, that Bazin attributes to the traditional realist artist. With the cinema, "the guiding myth . . . is the accomplishment of . . . an integral realism, a recreation of the world in its own image, an image unburdened by the freedom of interpretation of the artist or the irreversibility of time" (1: 21). Cinema becomes for Bazin an "asymptote of reality," just as fiction is for Joyce (2: 82). In both, there is some belief system imposed, but one in which Bazin and Joyce implicitly believe: a "revolutionary" or "fundamental humanism," as Bazin calls it (2: 21). The parallels become clearer as Bazin rhetorically asks, "Is not neorealism primarily a kind of humanism and only secondarily a style of film-making? Then as to the style itself, is it not essentially a form of self-effacement before reality?" (1: 29). Such statements remind one of the epiphanic doctrine of Stephen Daedalus: "it was for the man of letters to record these epiphanies with extreme care, seeing that they themselves are the most delicate and evanescent of moments" (*Stephen Hero*, 211).

While the Ballast office clock from *Stephen Hero* certainly represents "an item in the catalogue of Dublin's street furniture" (211), all the particulars of Dublin included in Joyce's work accomplish much more than that. For Joyce and Bazin both phenomenology and immanence (in the theological sense of a manifestation of the divine) are important: both of these realisms take "care not to cheat on reality, not only by contriving to give the succession of events the appearance of an accidental and as it were anecdotal chronology but in treating each of them according to its phenomenological integrity" (Bazin, 2: 51). As Bazin suggests, "realism subordinates what it borrows from reality to its transcendent needs. Neorealism knows only immanence" (2: 64). The neorealists and Joyce look upon the material world, each seeing and recreating a spiritual reality, be it the humanist religiosity sought and praised by André Bazin or the artistic transubstantiations of James Joyce.

In defending Rossellini's work, Bazin also reminds us that the director claims

> a love not only for his characters but for the real world just as it lies at the heart of his conception of the way film is to be directed, and that it is precisely this love that precludes him from putting asunder what reality has joined together, namely, the character and the setting. (2: 97-98)

Joyce also demonstrates such a love in his works, revering the divinely determined matrimonial union of character and place (with, of course, Joyce as the deity of his creation—the "Great Shapesphere," in the idiom of *Finnegans Wake* [295.04]). In all of Joyce's fiction, even in the apparently unrealistic world of *Finnegans Wake*, character and setting are inseparable. Joe Hynes of "Ivy Day in the Committee Room" cannot be understood apart from the precincts and the politics of Dublin. Without reference to Cork and to Clongowes, Stephen Dedalus's portrayal would be woefully incomplete. The pubs and churches, the theaters and restaurants create much of the character of Dublin and its inhabitants in *Ulysses*. And in *Finnegans Wake*, the geographically and historically real underlie the archetypal: Browne & Nolan, Booksellers and Stationers stand in for Giordano Bruno of Nola, and the Franciscan church of Adam and Eve's along the Liffey evoke the earlier couple, introducing the fall on the work's first page. The real consistently bolsters and anchors the Joycean fictional world.

A very different aspect of realism must be considered when comparing Walther Ruttmann's avant-garde documentary, *Berlin: The*

Symphony of A City (1927), to Joyce's work, especially *Ulysses*. This motion picture shows clear parallels to Joyce's fiction—correspondences that the author himself acknowledged by suggesting that Ruttmann could direct a film adaptation of *Ulysses*.[3] The film presents a day in the life of the German capital, creating a rhythmic portrait of the metropolis. But not only the film's obvious similarity with Joyce's rendering of diurnal urban life is important here. In both works, the documentary impulse, that move to depict physical reality is exalted, yet it is falsified and enhanced by the artificer; the audience senses that they encounter a mimesis of a city, but it is in fact no more real than a series of *trompe l'oeil* paintings. *Berlin* has been criticized by German film critic Siegfried Kracauer for overemphasizing the formal relationships between images, its "preoccupation with mental rather than physical reality," and its superimposition upon reality of "a network of ornamental relationships that tend to substitute for the things from which they are derived"—distinctions that all but disappear from a post-structural perspective (207). But just as *Berlin* does not present the photographic reality of the German capital, the Dublin of 1904 would not precisely resemble the city as rebuilt from Joyce's works. This remains the case in spite of Joyce's much vaunted aspirations: "I want," he told Frank Budgen, "to give a picture of Dublin so complete that if the city one day suddenly disappeared from the earth it could be reconstructed out of my book" (67–8). But Joyce's urban representation is not a piece of absolutely accurate photorealism, no matter how exact his portrayal often seems.

Both Joyce and Ruttmann create art through a reconstitution of the real, which evolves from a parallel modernist impulse to create a (not *the*) perception of reality. Ezra Pound admired the *Großstadt Symphony*, as the film is also known, for its "difficulty" and its "obscurity." With the appearance of *Berlin*, Pound observed in *The Exile* that "the machine film, the 'abstract' or Gestalt film now exists." The film "will take serious aesthetic criticism"; it is "in the [modernist] movement, and that should flatten out the opposition (to Joyce, to me . . .) with steamrolling ease and commodity" (114–115).

Pound's hyperbolic expectations may not have come true, but his comments about the film suggest the similarities of the two artists. One would inevitably expect parallels between two portraits of modern cities, but the vision is remarkably similar—the semblances of conception and execution strike one in many ways. With both, the audience finds art within the actual, or, more precisely, the actual can be made artistic. Ruttmann's earlier work, his animated shorts, *Lichtspiel, Opus I–IV* ("Lightplay," the contemporary German term for a film) suggest with their titles the influence not only of cinema, but also of music. However, their content emphasizes abstraction; geometric shapes undulate and move across the screen, invading the frame, creating the "rhythm in painting" for which Ruttmann and his mentor in painting and cinema, Viking Eggeling, were striving. With *Berlin*, such shapes are found and exposed within the urban environment; the real becomes abstract and archetypal (or prototypical), serving as raw material for the artist's vision and artifact. Joyce and Ruttmann alter their "real" cities to represent principles of universalism in shape and substance, behavior and actions.

Both *Ulysses* and *Berlin* offer a picture of a throbbing commercial metropolis—to paraphrase Bloom (and Joyce), "everything underlined" about the city is presented (*Ulysses*, 18.1177). All walks and aspects of life form a part of the portrait: the transportation system, the advertisements (both stationary and mobile), the shop windows, the entertainment venues, the newspapers, the bars and pubs, death and funerals, dawn and dusk, sun and rain. Just as Stephen Daedalus suggests to Cranly "that the clock of the Ballast Office was capable of an epiphany" as rendered by the spiritual perception and execution of the artist, so may a theater marquee reflected in a rain-washed street manifest itself for Ruttmann (*Stephen Hero*, 211).

There are also parallels of presentation and montage in the two works. A number of scenes will strike a chord of recognition in anyone familiar with *Ulysses*: the lunch scene in *Berlin* features montages intercutting between images of humans and animals eating, utilizing much the same method as "Lestrygonians"; the newspaper sections of each urban portrait prominently feature the headlines as a means to capture attention with their banners—in Ruttmann's work, they spin toward the viewer on an otherwise dark screen commanding the spectator's notice, just as they grab the eyes of Joyce's reader as he/she proceeds from the expected typography of "Hades" to the surprising layout of "Aeolus"; human advertisements walk through the streets of both municipalities—the sandwich board men promoting Wisdom Hely's stationery shop and the carnivalesque placard-bearing "giants" in Ruttmann's city "advertising a brand of epsom salts" (Minden, 207).

In his essay, "The City in Early Cinema: *Metropolis, Berlin*, and

October," Michael Minden observes some important features of Ruttmann's work which also bear relevance to *Ulysses*. These characteristics extend beyond the similarities in documentary content. For instance, one finds in both a tendency toward self-reflexivity or metadiscourse; as Minden describes Ruttmann's work, this quality becomes apparent:

> Berlin is documentary in style. But its true subject is not only Berlin, but, and perhaps more prominently, itself showing Berlin. Each choice of image, duration of shot, each camera angle and each montage juxtaposition reveals and shows itself, at the same time as it records a moment in the life of a busy Berlin day. (201)

Joyce's novel, while only partly documentary in style (most obviously in portions of "Wandering Rocks" and "Ithaca"), is frequently documentary in content, having often been regarded as an encyclopedic view of Dublin on Bloomsday. But clearly its subject is also the novel showing itself as it presents the city: with its self-referentiality—the novel even refers to itself in "Sirens" (e.g., "as said before")—and its altering of perspectives by the use of eighteen different techniques. Each chapter's style, each view of Dublin, and each alteration of narrative voice shows *itself*, emphasizing the ever-changing human aspect in the perception and interpretation of experience as well as underscoring that the audience views an artist's presentation.

Berlin and *Ulysses* also highlight for the audience the mechanized world of the city. Just as *Ulysses* refers to itself, one scene of Ruttmann's film shows a group of people being filmed; in his essay, Minden extrapolates from this scene, analyzing its importance:

> The point here, however, is that this ironic self-reflection incorporates and understands the medium of film as part of the multifarious range of machinery which constitutes an important part of the reality of the city. It classifies it alongside the factory machinery, typewriters and the telephone system as a component of an actual infrastructure. . . . [There is an] awareness of the cinema as having a part in the real and complex life of the city, its complex web of social, economic, imaginative determinations. (201)

These aspects of the piece may well have been what moved Pound to regard *Berlin* as a "machine film"; but the significance of such a genre should not be underestimated. Both the novel and the film present the mechanized portion of the cities, one of the aspects that make them modern and adds to their documentary character.

Throughout *Ulysses*, but especially in "Aeolus," technology forms a part of the new urban landscape—the tram system, the telephone and the telegraph, and the newspaper presses and the folding machines. Film, in Joyce's city, is conspicuous by its absence; but one suspects only because it was absent in reality in Dublin—with the Volta Cinematograph, Joyce himself established the first permanent picture house in Ireland in 1909. In 1904, cinema had only appeared in Erin in the form of mutoscopes (as Bloom reminds us in "Nausicaa") and traveling shows.

But film and the metropolis seem inextricably yoked: with *Ulysses*, Joyce creates an urban mimesis by using cinematic form; *Berlin*, with its conspicuous editing, also reminds one of the correlation between film form and the modern city. As Minden suggests:

> Film is . . . at home in the city because, used in a certain way, montage can approximate to the visual experience of being in a city. . . . [W]here the juxtaposition of moving images is not subordinated to a plot, and where the cuts are apparent, rather than hidden in the folds of a flowing narrative, the effect can be like the subjective experience of the city, namely a succession of different images and angles constructing a perception radically more rapid and less continuous than that encouraged by the traditional forms of literature, sculpture and painting. We are reminded of the words of Ezra Pound . . . : "the life of the village is narrative . . . In the city the visual impressions succeed each other, overlap, overcross, they are cinematographic."
>
> Whereas traditional forms have to break themselves up in order to achieve this sort of perception . . . , the cinema is constitutionally able to work with this sort of medium or language. (203)

What might be regarded as the cinematographic form in literature—the combination of abrupt transitions within streams-of-consciousness and those swift transformations of perspective, point-of-view and location that comprise *Ulysses*—provides a means to present the modern perception of an overwhelming urban environment.

The techniques of modernism, be they utilized in literature or cinema, may be employed to render the multiple perspectives and views that the complexities of the modern city and the modern consciousness require. What Minden notes about Ruttmann's film applies equally to Joyce's novel. The director and his associates

> do come up . . . against a fundamental problem associated with the artistic representation of modern cities. It is one of perspective. On one level Ruttmann's whole depersonalising strategy of montage recognises clearly, and successfully articulates, the problematic relationship between an individual and a city. The city is incommensurate with an individual's experience; overload is the key, the spiral. (207)

It is a similar realization about Dublin and modernist multi-perspectivism that moves Joyce to utilize the eighteen styles of the individual episodes and to employ parallax as not only *topos* and technique, but also as motif and theme throughout the novel.

In numerous ways then, Ruttmann's *Berlin* shares much of the external and perceptual qualities of Joyce's *Ulysses*, both as documentary and aesthetic creations. The German could have readily adapted many of these aspects of the novel to the screen, but as will be demonstrated in the next chapter, Eisenstein's ability to render the internal and the psychological on film made him an equally obvious choice for directing a screen adaptation of the novel, revealing an entirely different realm of the cinematic element in Joyce's fiction.

The relationship between the cinema and external reality is a complex one, as is the link between Joyce's fiction and the realistic film. His works clearly demonstrate important affinities to documentary and neorealist cinema, with all their attendant complexities. As with documentaries, be they dramatic as those of Flaherty or as stylized as Ruttmann's portrait of Berlin, the realistic aspects of Joyce's novels are tailored to an artistic vision. Like both the neorealists and many documentarians, Joyce recreates a specific social reality. Yet in recording the epiphanies of Dublin, the author also imbues his mimetic art with spiritual qualities, albeit from an unorthodox Joycean perspective; as with Bazin's neorealists, the world's transcendent qualities are made manifest through realistic fiction, not imposed upon it in the manner of the naturalists. Thus Joyce's use of the realistic aspects throughout his canon can be better understood if one keeps in mind not only the devices that offer nature "the power to reproduce herself" and permit the creation of "an integral realism, a recreation of the world in its own image" but also their important implications for art and aesthetics, for a perception and representation of the modernist world.

NOTES

[1] This type of aesthetic inquiry can be found in a slightly altered form in Stephen's disquisitions to Lynch in Chapter V of *Portrait*: "*Can excrement or a child or a louse be a work of art? If not, why not? . . . If a man hacking in fury at a block of wood,* Stephen continued, *make there an image of a cow, is that image a work of art? If not, why not?*" (214).

[2] Compare Joyce, *The Critical Writings*, 141n for Flaubert's original formulation, from a letter to Mlle. Leroyer de Chantepie, March 18, 1857: "L'artiste doit être dans son oeuvre comme Dieu dans la Création, invisible et tout-puissant, qu'on le sente partout, mais qu'on le voie pas."

[3] Ruttmann reportedly spent time in Paris in the 1920s and knew Phillipe Soupault. I have not, however, been able to discover if he knew Joyce or was familiar with his work.

CHAPTER FOUR
In the Linguistic Kitchen
Joyce, Eisenstein and Cinema Language

> Here is the savage economy of hiero-glyphics. Here words are not the polite contortions of 20th century printer's ink. They are alive. They elbow their way on to the page, and glow and blaze and fade and disappear.
>
> —Samuel Beckett, on *Work in Progress* in "Dante... Bruno. Vico.. Joyce"
>
> The true material of the sound-film is . . . the monologue.
>
> —Eisenstein, "A Course in Treatment"

One of the names most often associated with Joyce and the cinematic aspects of his work is the great Russian director and film theorist, Sergei Eisenstein. Eisenstein frequently prescribed Joyce's fiction as required reading for young filmmakers, and he refers to Joyce often in his theoretical essays. In one essay he mentions Joyce only once (and then in a footnote), yet two important concepts emerge which relate to the Irishman's work. While "The Cinematographic Principle and the Ideogram," an exploration of montage and Japanese culture, may seem an unlikely place from which to begin a discussion on Joyce, Eisenstein's synthetic mind perceives common elements of cinematography in modern literature, ancient calligraphy and Japanese art.[1] Nor would this connection have surprised Joyce himself. In her "Meetings with Joyce," Dr. Carola Giedion-Welcker recalls the writer's reaction to a Japanese translation of *Ulysses*:

When the Japanese edition of Ulysses appeared in 1932, he showed it to me with special interest. He believed that, because the Japanese mentality was used to an indirect and fragmentary symbol language and also because their form of poetic expression was close to his, they were well prepared for his way of thinking and writing. (Potts, 266)

That Joyce identified his art with ideogrammatic expression is certainly clear from his later use of the "letterwords" or the sigla used in *Finnegans Wake*: "The Doodles family, ⋔,△,⊣,✕,☐,∧ Hoodle doodle fam.?" (299. Note 4).² In a letter to Harriet Shaw Weaver, he seems taken with some linguistic coincidences regarding the first siglum, supplied to him, which designates HCE and Finn MacCool: "A Chinese student sent me some letterwords I had Iaskedfor. The last one is ⛰ . It means 'mountain' and is called 'Chin', the common people's way of pronouncing Hin or Fin" (*Letters* I, 250). Thus, considering the similarities between Joycean and Japanese art (as filtered through Eisenstein) will reveal some of the cinematic aspects of the former's work.

The first idea from Eisenstein's essay that must be examined in relation to Joyce's "cinematic" fiction is the ideogram. Eisenstein begins by explaining the prevalence of the cinematic concept of montage in Japanese culture while noting its complete absence in their cinema. He then offers a brief history of the ideogram, the foundation of Japanese writing, and explores its means of signification as well as its dual functions of denotation and depiction:

> The copulation (perhaps we had better say, the combination) of two hieroglyphs of the simplest series is to be regarded not as their sum, but as their product, i.e. as a value to another dimension, another degree; each, separately, corresponds to an *object*, to a fact, but their combination corresponds to a *concept*. From separate hieroglyphs has been fused—the ideogram. By combination of the two 'depictables' is achieved the representation of something that is graphically undepictable.

Eisenstein explains this process of hieroglyphic montage: "the picture of an ear near the drawing of a door = 'to listen'; . . . a mouth + a child = 'to scream'" (29–30).

In his short essay, "Joyce and Eisenstein: Literary Reflections on the Reel World," William Costanzo discusses Eisenstein's 1929 piece on the ideogram in connection with *Finnegans Wake*. In Joyce's last work, "signs denoting objects could be juxtaposed or superimposed to signify abstract ideas," similar to the method of both ideograms and montage. "Written language," as Costanzo suggests, "needed to be reinvented, recombined, reprocessed at the grass roots level of the word." As mentioned in Chapter One, Joyce "refashioned the pun in the image of montage": "like the Chinese word for East, which superimposes a picture of the sun on a picture of a tree . . . , [in the word "meanderthalltale,"] the combination of *neanderthal, meander*, and *me and the tall tale* challenges the mind to make connections, to synthesize the seemingly familiar into concepts that are yet to be explored" (177–79). Of course, the word "thrall" also lurks in the midst of this portmanteau.[3]

For Joyce, however, montage on the level of the word predates the composition of *Finnegans Wake*. At a very basic, and perhaps minor level, montage frequently occurs in *Dubliners* with compound words. The description of Maria's "grey-green eyes" in "Clay" and of the "peacock-blue muslin" scarf "wound round" the object of Farrington's longing glances in "Counterparts" cause the reader to combine these two terms (101, 95), creating "a sense or meaning not objectively contained in the images [or words] themselves but derived exclusively from their juxtaposition" (Bazin, 1: 25). In this case the two "depictables" combine to give a more accurate description—a tacit admission that one word alone cannot convey the idea. However, most of the compound nouns and adjectives in *Dubliners* remain hyphenated—generally conventional, they pass by unnoticed.

In *A Portrait of the Artist as a Young Man* one begins to observe the typically Joycean compounds, those unusual fusions of words which convention separates by a space or, failing that, the weak gesture of a hyphen. Those disappointed "grey-green" eyes of Maria become "the bristling greygreen weeds" of Stephen's hellish vision (137). The simple elimination of the hyphen suggests the inseparable aspect of the colors—as in montage, the description represents their product, not their sum. The two colors blend, suggesting the living death of this inferno and evoking a bleak eternal existence.

But in *A Portrait* Joyce does not use compounds simply for the gradations of hue or the descriptions of household objects as he does in *Dubliners*. The compounds increase in complexity and sophistication, achieving more power in combination. Expressions like Donovan's "small fatencircled eyes" and the captain's "monkey-puckered" face are savored as much because they are conjoined as they are for their cleverness (210, 227). Furthermore, compounds aid Joyce in his quest for veracity; in a way that a phrase might not capture, the word "flourfattened" simultaneously characterizes the quality of the gravy and the food for which Stephen hungers (102). The "rainsodden" earth's "mortal odour" of St. Stephen's Green and the "rainfragrant" hair of Stephen's sister yoke words to create images that are not only precise but also more evocative and sensual than they would be as separate entities (184, 228).

But only in *Ulysses* do the compounds begin to take on montage qualities, as Costanzo describes them. We move beyond the fusions of montage to the collisions of ideas achieving an abstract concept to be created by the reader as a part of the process of artistic perception. Eisenstein regarded montage fundamentally as a collision—with a "view that from the collision of two given factors *arises* a concept" (*Film Form*, 37). And in his essay "Word and Image" in *The Film Sense*, Eisenstein explains the audience's part in the process of art: "*A work of art, understood dynamically, is just this process of arranging images in the feelings and mind of the spectator*. It is this that constitutes the peculiarity of a truly vital work of art and distinguishes it from a lifeless one, in which the spectator receives the represented result of a given consummated process of creation, instead of being drawn into the process as it occurs" (17, emphasis added).[4] For example, elements clash to communicate ideas that one word alone cannot express—"beautifulinsadness" aptly describes Mr Best's complex emotions, while "*clipclaps glovesilent hands*" perfectly conjures the dandified Professor Maginni's cultured, muted applause for the dance of the morning and the noon hours (9.735, 15.4060). The onomatopoeic "*clipclaps*" also reminds one that Joyce frequently uses compounds for their imitative sounds in addition to the montage/collision of their sense. Furthermore, Joyce reveals important facets of Bloom's character through many of the descriptions given in "Circe": the "stage directions" depict him as a "*warmgloved, mammamufflered*" sixteen year old (15.3333). "*Warmgloved*" proffers an image of security and protection against the harmful elements; "*mammamufflered*" not only suggests the insulation of clothing, but also the source of this security and Bloom's dependence upon Ellen Bloom. Such images achieve an economy of expression; as Eisenstein notes of the ideogram, "when transposed into literary exposition [it] gives rise to . . . [a] laconism of pointed imagery" (31).

These combinations are artful, but neither is Joyce above using them to arouse disgust nor to be meanspirited. "Snotgreen," that "new art colour for our Irish poets," shows Joyce at his most frank, suggesting not only the state of Irish art, but also our bard's earthiness (1.73). In assessing the activities of the scholars in the library, Stephen comments: "Unwed, unfancied, ware of wiles, they fingerponder nightly each his variorum edition of *The Taming of the Shrew*" (9.1062–63). In such a sentence, in its entirety a series of fragmented montage images, the collocation "fingerponder" leads one to suspect onanism in the study.

Twice labeling Christ as "Agenbuyer"—in "Scylla and Charybdis" and "Oxen of the Sun" (9.494, 14.295)—Joyce creates a montage of the religious and the personal:[5] Christ truly is a "buyer of remorse," assuming the sins of the world; using this particular term explicitly echoes the connection with Stephen, the secular son carrying his burdensome Agenbite of Inwit. The compounds here begin to take on the complexity, if not the density of the word montage of *Finnegans Wake*; Joyce has begun to pack his portmanteaus. They increase in complexity and multiple meanings—some readers might say to the point of unpardonable confusion—once the author begins *Finnegans Wake*.

But montage and cinematographic techniques occur on other levels in Joyce's fiction as well. After establishing the basic principles of the ideogram in his essay, Eisenstein proceeds to discuss its relation to cinematic and literary form; as he explains, the ideogrammatic system is:

> a means and method inevitable in any cinematographic exposition. And, in a condensed and purified form, the starting point for the "intellectual" cinema . . . a cinema seeking a maximum laconism for the visual representation of abstract concepts . . . [that] when transposed into literary exposition, gives rise to an identical laconism of pointed imagery. . . . The same method, expanded into the luxury of a group of already formed verbal combinations, swells into a splendor of imagist effect. The concept is a bare formula; its adornment (an expansion by additional material) transforms the formula into an image—a finished form. (29–31)

The oriental influence upon imagism, from Ernest Fenollosa via Pound, and even Eisenstein's connections to the Japanese, are noted by Hugh Kenner in *The Pound Era* (162). Clearly this idea had a significant influence upon imagism and modernism, as Kenner suggests. But further investigation in connection with Joyce reveals more about the emotional power of his prose.

One of Eisenstein's observations regarding Japanese culture directly applies to Joyce, as the Russian director himself suggests in a note. Ideograms, he suggests, fuse denotative and depictive tendencies—they signify and they represent. And the latter aspect is evident in "the most perfect examples of Japanese pictorial art." Relying on his eclectic reading, Eisenstein quotes at length the observations of Julius Kurth on the art of the eighteenth century print maker Sharaku—the "Japanese Daumier." Comparing a wood-cut portrait and an antique Noh mask, Kurth notes:

> The faces of both the print and the mask wear an identical expression.... While the carved mask was constructed according to fairly accurate anatomical proportions, the proportions of the portrait print are simply impossible.... That the artist was unaware that all these proportions are false is, of course, out of the question. It was with a full awareness that he <u>repudiated normalcy, and, while the drawing of the separate features depends on severely concentrated naturalism, their proportions have been subordinated to purely intellectual considerations.</u> *He set up the essence of the psychic expression as the norm for the proportions of the single features.*[6]

Predictably, Eisenstein compares this distortion with that practiced in the cinema:

> Is this not exactly what we of the cinema do temporally, just as Sharaku in simultaneity, when we cause a monstrous disproportion of the parts of a normally flowing event, and suddenly dismember the event into 'close-up of clutching hands,' 'medium shots of the struggle,' and 'extreme close-up of bulging eyes,' in making a montage disintegration of the event in various planes? In making an eye twice as large as a man's full figure?! By combining these monstrous incongruities we newly collect the disintegrated event into one whole, but in our aspect. According to the treatment of our relation to the event.

This repudiation of normalcy and the subordination of naturalism—meaning realism in literary critical terms—to intellectual consideration and psychic expression, so common in the cinema, is directly linked by Eisenstein to Joyce in a note two pages later: "it has been left to James Joyce to develop in *literature* the depictive line of the Japanese hieroglyph. Every word of Kurth's analysis of Sharaku may be applied, neatly and easily, to Joyce" (33–35).

Even before Eisenstein mentions Joyce, these "monstrous incongruities" and "the disintegrated event into one whole, but in *our* aspect," along with the "monstrous disproportion of the parts of a normally flowing event" might recall episodes like "Cyclops" and

"Circe" to a Joycean reader of Eisenstein. But this principle may be observed, in a small but significant way, before we arrive at the point where the incongruities and disproportions become excessive. We can observe "the expressiveness of archaic disproportion," as Eisenstein calls it, in both *A Portrait* and the early portions of *Ulysses* (34–35). By archaic, Eisenstein means both the art of prehistory and the art of children, in which the proportions of images indicate their significance. He quotes from George Rowley's *Principles of Chinese Painting*, "in all ideational art, objects are given size according to their importance, the king being twice as large as his subjects, or a tree half the size of a man when it merely informs us that the scene is out-of-doors." But just as important, for Eisenstein, is what these "forms are set against—the expressiveness of archaic disproportion" is opposed to "absolutism" and the "regulated 'stone tables' of officially decreed harmony" (34).

In some ways the opening section of *A Portrait* perfectly exemplifies this archaic disproportion, and many sections of the novel indeed prefigure this technique that will flower in *Ulysses*. The incongruities may not be monstrous; nevertheless, the disproportion of a child's perception is clearly represented and the parts of a normally flowing event are chopped up to offer to the reader another aspect of the event—be it the author's and/or the protagonist's. Rather than consider this well-worn page, let us examine more fully a later portrait of Stephen Dedalus as a young poet.

Awakening with his soul "all dewy wet," Stephen begins the composition of his villanelle (217). But remembering the frustrations of his relationship with E_____ C_____, he is wrathful:

> Rude brutal anger routed the last lingering instant of ecstasy from his soul. It broke up violently her fair image and flung the fragments on all sides. On all sides distorted reflections of her image started from his memory: the flowergirl in the ragged dress with damp coarse hair and a hoyden's face who had called herself his own girl and begged his handsel, the kitchengirl in the next house who sang over the clatter of her plates with the drawl of a country singer the first bars of *By Killarney's Lakes and Fells*, a girl who had laughed gaily to see him stumble when the iron grating in the footpath near Cork Hill had caught the broken sole of his shoe, a girl he had glanced at, attracted by her small ripe mouth as she passed out of Jacob's biscuit factory, who had cried to him over her shoulder.

—Do you like what you seen of me, straight hair and curly eyebrows? (220)

Here, as Eisenstein suggests, we find that Joyce has repudiated normalcy to heighten the poet's emotions. Stephen's anger breaks the fair image of the beloved and hurls the fragments aside. The separate features do retain a realistic aspect, yet they represent the "distorted reflections of her image." As readers explore Stephen's memory and glimpse these likenesses, they realize that the separate parts of each of these women have been "subordinated to purely intellectual considerations"—the hair, face, voice and laugh of the young lady, even her mouth, are twisted to meet Stephen's angry end. The young artist transforms his love into a series of women who are, by turns, coarse and ragged, rural and low in station, boisterous and saucy, taunting and teasing. The memories of the inamorata become perverted to these lower creatures as Stephen metes out his mental punishment for E____ C____'s betrayal. Here, the "essence of psychic expression" has become the norm; the women are combined in a vulgar montage to cheapen the image of the beloved, to sully her purity. Representing the vision of Stephen's ire, a disintegration of the person in various planes occurs, so as to collect the fragments into a whole that communicates his angered aspect. His retribution against her is thus offered in a powerful cinematographic presentation.

In *Ulysses*, this filmic technique of deformation recurs even in the first episodes of both the "Telemachiad" and the "Wanderings of Ulysses." In *Ulysses*, the cinematic prose is more fragmented than the narrator-mediated access to Stephen's mind in *A Portrait*; Joyce moves from indirect to direct interior monologue. Stephen's memories of his mother, precipitated by Buck Mulligan's mention of his aunt's accusations of matricide, offer an interesting example. Here Joyce presents another vision of the aesthete and poet:

> Stephen, an elbow rested on the jagged granite, leaned his palm against his brow and gazed at the fraying edge of his shiny black coatsleeve. Pain, that was not yet the pain of love, fretted his heart. Silently, in a dream she had come to him after her death, her wasted body within its loose brown graveclothes giving off an odour of wax and rosewood, her breath, that had bent upon him, mute, reproachful, a faint odour of wetted ashes. Across the threadbare cuffedge he saw the sea hailed as a great sweet mother by the wellfed voice beside him. The ring of bay and skyline held a dull green mass of liquid. A bowl of white china had stood beside

her deathbed holding the green sluggish bile which she had torn up from her rotting liver by fits of loud groaning vomiting. (1.100–110)[7]

As Stephen's mother appears to him, the gruesome details are presented. But their proportions have been subordinated to Stephen's own memories of the dream—he recalls primarily the smell of his mother's body and breath, only briefly remarking on the sight of her wasted body within those graveclothes. These particulars underscore the guilt of Stephen's refusal to kneel as he feels the slight pressure of her mute, reproachful breath and smells the "odour of wetted ashes" of a penitent. The strength of these visions cause olfactory memories, suggesting how the dream haunts all of Stephen's senses, even when he averted his eyes during the nightmare.

In this selection we also find the repudiation of normalcy: while the "wellfed voice" can acknowledge the sea as sweet mother and appreciate the humor of its snotgreen color, Stephen transmutes the bay into the bedside bowl with its bilious discharge. The change presents an incongruity, one determined by the psyche of the perceiver, as well as monstrous disproportion—the bowl looms as large as the bay with all its massive bitterness weighing upon the mourning, irreligious son. Within this paragraph we find the disintegration of the event into various planes. What begins as reverie upon the sea becomes the disintegrated memories of Stephen, uniting finally in one whole presenting Stephen's regret and guilt.

Although Stephen's mood soon alters slightly, both it and the cinematic technique continue when Buck Mulligan's taunts, along with his ironic rendering of a verse of Yeats's song, call forth bittersweet memories for the young Dedalus:

> A cloud began to cover the sun slowly, wholly, shadowing the bay in deeper green. It lay beneath him, a bowl of bitter waters. Fergus' song: I sang it alone in the house, holding down the long dark chords. Her door was open: she wanted to hear my music. Silent with awe and pity I went to her bedside. She was crying in her wretched bed. For those words, Stephen: love's bitter mystery.
>
> Where now?
>
> Her secrets: old featherfans, tasselled dancecards, powdered with musk, a gaud of amber beads in her locked drawer. A birdcage hung in the sunny window of her house when she was a girl. She heard old Royce sing in the pantomime of *Turko the Terrible* and laughed with others when he sang:

> I am the boy
>
> That can enjoy
>
> Invisibility.
>
> Phantasmal mirth, folded away: muskperfumed.
>
> And no more turn aside and brood.
>
> Folded away in the memory of nature with her toys. Memories beset his brooding brain. Her glass of water from the kitchen tap when she had approached the sacrament. A cored apple, filled with brown sugar, roasting for her at the hob on a dark autumn evening. Her shapely fingernails reddened by the blood of squashed lice from the children's shirts.
>
> In a dream, silently she had come to him, her wasted body... (1.248–70)

The cloud darkens both the mood and the bitterness, deepening the green still more; and Stephen's expansion of bay to bowl becomes unequivocal with the second sentence. The remainder of the first paragraph presents a vision of Stephen and his mother interacting. But these depicted memories halt with Stephen's ambiguous question regarding either the location of his mother's soul or her "secrets."

In a manner reminiscent of *haiku*, with its "indirect and fragmentary symbol language," Joyce begins to unveil for us in a series of disintegrated images the essence of May Dedalus as her son regarded her. Where now are her secrets, those which were treasured as signs of youth and love? Her psyche is exposed by the small details of the locked drawer presented laconically to express her character. The next sentence moves us quickly, discontinuously back beyond the youthful dancer to the little girl's memories of birdsong and sun-filled rooms. Finally the joy of laughter is captured by a memory of Old Royce singing "the most successful [song] in the whole book" of a much-lauded musical comedy (Thornton, 17). These memories, though disintegrated, present a whole of "mirth," uniting the parts of the event of Stephen's brooding, as he mourns over lost joys. Stephen's dream of his mother's visit from beyond the grave will resume as soon as Stephen mentally closes the drawer containing all these happier times. That illusory joy, that "phantasmal mirth" will be "folded away in the memory of nature with her toys"—the musk perfume and the sweet roasting apple soon to be replaced by her smell from the grave. Remembering the killing of the lice, Stephen returns to his brooding on death and its hold over him. The psychic expression of Stephen's joy as expressed in these images is halted by a disgusting and apparently incongruous vision; a montage/collision of his mother killing vermin and the mother whom he "killed" returns Stephen to his morning's touchstone.

One might here consider Joyce's comments regarding Japanese poetic language given earlier. After his general remarks as reported by Giedion-Welcker, she recalls Joyce's specific example:

> A Japanese poem which he recited to me in English translation showed the different 'I's,' which changed according to the situation. It dealt with an abandoned sweetheart whose multifaceted and fluctuating psychic state was expressed through symbolic allusions (mist, clouds, jewels, etc.) thereby also revealing the personality of the lamenting sweetheart. (Potts, 266)

This is precisely the vision of Stephen we receive—his "multifaceted and fluctuating psychic state" is expressed through symbolic allusions and symbolic items. With Stephen, of course, we have maternal abandonment, but Joyce expresses it in much the same way as the Japanese poet he admired.

Just as he has given us a glimpse into the melancholy Stephen, Joyce employs a similar technique as he presents two sides of Bloom early on that same morning. Here Joyce, as in so many places in *Ulysses,* offers readers the psychic expression of a character by presenting a series of incongruous events—a glimpse of the mental aspects of an event, a simple top-of-the-morning walk in Dublin, as we follow Bloom through the bright June day to the butcher's:

> He crossed to the bright side, avoiding the loose cellarflap of number seventyfive. The sun was nearing the steeple of George's church. Be a warm day I fancy. Specially in these black clothes feel it more. Black conducts, reflects, (refracts is it?), the heat. But I couldn't go in that light suit. Make a picnic of it. His eyelids sank quietly often as he walked in the happy warmth. Boland's breadvan delivering with trays our daily but she prefers yesterday's loaves turnovers crisp crowns hot. Makes you feel young. Somewhere in the east: early morning: set off at dawn. Travel round in front of the sun, steal a day's march on him. Keep it up for ever never grow a day older technically. Walk along a strand, strange land, come to a city gate, sentry there, old ranker too, old Tweedy's big moustaches, leaning on a long kind of a spear.

> Wander through awned streets. Turbaned faces going by. Dark caves of carpet shops, big man, Turko the terrible, seated cross-legged, smoking a coiled pipe. Cries of sellers in the streets. Drink water scented with fennel, sherbet. Dander along all day. Might meet a robber or two. Well, meet him. Getting on to sundown. The shadows of the mosques along the pillars: priest with a scroll rolled up. A shiver of the trees, signal, the evening wind. I pass on. Fading gold sky. A mother watches me from her doorway. She calls her children home in their dark language. High wall: beyond strings twanged. Night sky, moon, violet, colour of Molly's new garters. Strings. Listen. A girl playing one of those instruments what do you call them: dulcimers. I pass.
>
> Probably not a bit like it really. Kind of stuff you read: in the track of the sun. Sunburst on the titlepage. (4.77–100)

Here, we begin with the bright sun and "the happy warmth" which make one feel youthful and impart a buoyant quality to all of Bloom's surroundings. Bloom quickly proceeds, through his usual discontinuous interior monologue, to the breadvan and then to his romantic vision of the East, with a small detour to consider the physics of time and aging in his eccentric and whimsically scientific way. A series of stereotypical images creates his montage view of the East with its hookahs and markets, its danger and sensuality. The series of laconic images combine to create a swelling of an imagist vision of the East. We take a measure of the Orient which resembles that of the Araby bazaar while we also take stock of the character who has this vision. He finds himself entangled in this quaint scene and gaining confidence within it—taking on even the robbers and recalling his wife's new garters, violet as his fantasy sky. Bloom's vision of the East clearly reveals his psyche. The particulars of his reverie suggest his preoccupations, recreating his aspect: his fears counteracted by a burst of hopeful confidence, his sensuality and fetishism, his affection for motherhood, his penchant for romance, all from his memories, both from personal experience and popular literature.

But such ecstacy must elude the ever practical Bloom, who readily concedes that the east is not a "bit like it really" and he must "pass." Even this realization takes a montage turn: he moves from the clichéd "in the track of the sun" to the visual "sunburst on the titlepage." The same idea finds expression in two ways, each reinforced by collision with the other and both demonstrating the bent of Bloom's mind and reading. The happy and sensuous reverie, created from this disintegrated, but ultimately unified, montage of the east, gives way to the realities of Dublin: its porter, its politics and its commercial possibilities. The pieces of the montage recompose into a whole, providing us a glimpse into Leopold Bloom.

Yet not all of Bloom's persona is revealed in even this dense a passage. Joyce offers the gloomier cast of Bloom's mind in his reaction to that same darkening of the sky that brought Stephen such bitter memories:

> A cloud began to cover the sun slowly, wholly.
>
> Grey. Far.
>
> No, not like that. A barren land, bare waste, Vulcanic lake, the dead sea: no fish, weedless, sunk deep in the earth. No wind could lift those waves, grey metal, poisonous foggy waters. Brimstone they called it raining down: the cities of the plain: Sodom, Gomorrah, Edom. All dead names. A dead sea in a dead land, grey and old. Old now. It bore the oldest, the first race. A bent hag crossed from Cassidy's, clutching a naggin bottle by the neck. The oldest people. Wandered far away over all the earth, captivity to captivity, multiplying, dying, being born everywhere. It lay there now. Now it could bear no more. Dead: an old woman's: the grey sunken cunt of the world.
>
> Desolation.
>
> Grey horror seared his flesh. Folding the page into his pockets he turned into Eccles street, hurrying homeward. Cold oils slid along his veins, chilling his blood: age crusting him with a salt cloak. Well, I am here now. Yes, I am here now. Morning mouth bad images. Got up wrong side of the bed. Must begin again those Sandow's exercises. On the hands down. (4.218–34)

This passage is perhaps even more discontinuous than the other examples. The jumps can be logically traced, but at least on an initial reading they are incongruous, disproportionate and again remind one of Joyce's comments upon Japanese language: "an indirect and fragmentary symbol language." Numerous quick changes of topic occur in the interior monologue; the Bloomian manner of cinematographic thinking is evident.

Even in the first paragraph of the passage, the laconism of the cinema language can be seen: "slowly, wholly. Grey. Far." The descriptions work in a montage manner, colliding with one another to express the dramatic nature of the greyness that the cloud creates. With the next burst of thought ("No, not like that."), Bloom recalls his earlier vision of the romantic East. Having assumed that the reality could not rival his oriental dream, he now readily concedes how far it falls short of his imaginary creation. He illustrates this deficiency with a series of glimpses of the sterile east: a dead, barren wasteland with neither fish nor even weeds. Such a vision causes him to picture the destruction of the cities of the plain: old, ruined, dead. This then takes Bloom back to the origins of humanity and of the Jews. To use Eisenstein's terms, an imagist effect is created by an "adornment (an expansion by additional material)" leading to the paradox of a depressing "splendor" (31). We find these images interrupted with the appearance of the old, bent Irish woman, seizing her small whisky bottle—then quickly switching to the diaspora and the final, infertile image. It is described by its qualities first, creating an aura of chilling depression: the dead, old, "grey sunken cunt of the world." The infertility and death of the east is transformed into a bodily image, shrinking and concentrating it, providing a disproportionate picture—the reciprocal of the relationship between the bowl and the bay in "Telemachus."

After the summation of all these pictures into one concentrated word and paragraph, a simple image or emotion ("Desolation"), we discover Bloom's assessment of and reaction to the situation. With chilled blood, he recalls the fate of Lot's wife (see Gifford, 75). The East of oranges has transformed to one of divine retribution because of "morning mouth," getting out of bed on the wrong side, or a lack of exercise. Or it may just be the quick disappearance of the sun. No matter the cause of Bloom's dampened spirits, Joyce has provided us with another view to the psychic expression of a character with a series of incongruities and disproportions—subordinating the realistic picture of the morning to the psyche of the individual, uniting the disintegrated events and imaginings into a whole of the character's aspect, a psychological portrait—of the barrenness of a Jew without a son, an estranged husband, an outcast.

It should come as little surprise that Eisenstein's suggestion bears fruit, that Joyce develops "in *literature* the depictive line of the Japanese hieroglyph." As the director himself recognized, in "the linguistic kitchen of literature, Joyce occupies himself with the same thing I rave about in relation to laboratory researches on cinema language" (*Immoral Memories*, 213). From Joyce's early stories, in which he combined words to multiply their effect, to the collisions of words and the grotesqueries of psychic disproportion in *Ulysses*, on through the complexities crammed into the overstuffed portmanteaus of *Finnegans Wake*, the cinematic language of Eisenstein can be discerned.

NOTES

[1] In her study, *James Joyce: The Poetry Of Conscience*, (Milwaukee: Inland Press, 1961), Mary Parr briefly discusses the relevance of this essay to *Ulysses*, but she does not pursue the connections that I discuss here. As discussed on p. 50–51, William Costanzo's essay, "Joyce and Eisenstein: Literary Reflections on the Reel World," also relies on this essay and is more relevant to my discussion.

[2] As Roland McHugh notes these symbols were used by Joyce in his manuscripts for characters and principles in the novel, "respectively, Earwicker, Anna, Issy, the 4 old men, the title of the book, Shaun & Shem" (299).

[3] As Professor Jack Kolb has suggested to me.

[4] See also Costanzo, 178.

[5] While in some ways the examples here could be considered as motifs or echoes, the concept of montage permits one to posit an interaction, a collision between the parts of the words and expressions that lead us to a third term, that new understanding which we as reader/audience create by our interpretation of this collision.

[6] Eisenstein's own italics are reproduced throughout this chapter; here I have underscored certain portions to provide my own emphasis.

[7] Robert Ryf also analyzes this passage in terms of its filmic technique. But his primary concern is with superimposition—obviously a concern here—not with the technique as it reveals the character and the repudiation of normalcy. The passages that I analyze certainly represent the interior monologues of the characters; however, I believe the selection and presentation of these monologues can also be discussed in light of film techniques. In his book, *The Stream of Consciousness and Beyond in* Ulysses, Erwin Steinberg considers film as one of the sources of the stream of consciousness technique but does not pursue this connection.

CHAPTER FIVE
Cinema Fakes
Film and Joycean Fantasy

> The act which in the ordinary theater would go on in our mind alone is ... in the photoplay projected into the pictures themselves. It is as if reality has lost its own continuous shape and become shaped by the demands of our soul.
>
> —Hügo Munsterburg

> Cinema fakes, drown, state of sea, tank, steeplejack, steeple on floor, camera above; jumps 10 feet, 1 foot camera in 6 foot pit.
>
> — "Circe," Scribbledehobble

As Joyce laid aside the beginnings of *Ulysses* to compose *Exiles* in 1915, one of the first American studies of the cinema appeared. A consideration of the relationship between Joyce and film cannot ignore Vachel Lindsay's eccentric book on the photoplay, *The Art of the Moving Picture*, as it bears particular relevance to the more fantastic aspects of Joyce's cinematic techniques and aesthetics: the representation of dreams, visions and hallucinations.[1] Moving beyond the psychic disproportion of Eisenstein discussed in the previous chapter, one ought to study the similarity of these proto-surrealist portions of Joyce's fiction to what David Bordwell has called one of the "founts of cinema": the filmic fantasy exemplified by the trick films of Georges Méliès and other lesser known movie magicians such as Leopoldo Fregoli, who on stage and film entertained audiences by swiftly transforming himself into a succession of different characters seemingly instantaneously, and G. Wilhelm ("Billy") Bitzer, later renowned as D. W. Griffith's cinematographer. While in the third chapter I considered some of the misleading aspects of documentary realism as they relate to Joyce's narratives, this chapter concerns the opposite: the fantastic elements of cinematic tricks spliced between the realistic aspects of Joyce's fiction.

As a point of departure, one cannot help but acknowledge the conventionality of the dreams and visions in the early fiction—no matter how effective they may be, the phantasms of the night in *Dubliners* follow traditional paths; the events of the dreams seem little different from daylight activities. In "The Sisters," the boy envisions the deceased Father Flynn in his bedroom:

> In the dark of my room I imagined that I saw again the heavy grey face of the paralytic. I drew the blankets over my head and tried to think of Christmas. But the grey face still followed me. It murmured; and I understood that it desired to confess something. I felt my soul receding into some pleasant and vicious region; and there again I found it waiting for me. It began to confess to me in a murmuring voice and I wondered why it smiled continually and why the lips were so moist with spittle. (11)

The next day, the boy no longer recalls so many particulars from the dream—it has slipped back into the recesses of the unconscious, never to be fully experienced by the reader, as are the more painstakingly recreated and vividly described dreams in Joyce's later works. The boy tries "to remember what had happened afterwards in the dream. I remembered that I had noticed long velvet curtains and a swinging lamp of antique fashion. I felt that I had been very far away, in some land where the customs were strange—in Persia, I thought. . . . But I could not remember the end of the dream" (13–14).

Likewise, Gabriel's reverie at the close of "The Dead," though detailed, somber and heart-rending, assumes a conventional, almost mundane, form:

> Poor Aunt Julia! She, too, would soon be a shade with the shade of Patrick Morkan and his horse. . . . Soon, perhaps, he would be sitting in that same drawing-room, dressed in black, his silk hat on his knees. The blinds would be drawn down and Aunt Kate would be sitting beside him, crying and blowing her nose and telling him how Julia had died. He would cast about in his mind for some words that might console her, and would find only lame and useless ones.

. . .

Cinema Fakes: Film and Joycean Fantasy

> The tears gathered more thickly in his eyes and in the partial darkness he imagined he saw the form of a young man standing under a dripping tree. Other forms were near. His soul had approached that region where dwell the vast hosts of the dead. He was conscious of, but could not apprehend, their wayward and flickering existence. His own identity was fading out into a grey and impalpable world: the solid world itself which these dead had one time reared and lived in was dissolving and dwindling. (222–23)

Gabriel's description of the afterlife contains nearly as many clichés as his toast to Irish hospitality after his aunts' dinner. Even Stephen's fevered prophetic visions of Parnell's funeral procession as the youngster languishes in the infirmary in the first chapter of *A Portrait of the Artist as a Young Man* represent a relatively tame dream sequence, compared with the bizarre grotesqueries of *Ulysses* and *Finnegans Wake*.

Only in Stephen's vision of hell do we begin to receive a sense of a dream logic and the personae of the unconscious, of the fantasy that is to come in the later novels:

> Creatures were in the field; one, three, six: creatures were moving in the field, hither and thither. Goatish creatures with human faces, hornybrowed, lightly bearded and grey as indiarubber. The malice of evil glittered in their hard eyes, as they moved hither and thither, trailing their long tails behind them. A rictus of cruel malignity lit up greyly their old bony faces. One was clasping about his ribs a torn flannel waistcoat, another complained monotonously as his beard stuck in the tufted weeds. Soft language issued from their spittleless lips as they swished in slow circles round and round the field, winding hither and thither through the weeds, dragging their long tails amid the rattling canisters. They moved in slow circles, circling closer and closer to enclose, to enclose, soft language issuing from their lips, their long swishing tails besmeared with stale shite, thrusting upwards their terrific faces . . . (137–38)

These sinful satyrs augur beings in the nightmare of "Circe," the goats dressed and speaking as humans reminding one of the talking animals and props of that episode. Combining sin and guilt in an archetypal form, clad in tatters, their tails covered with feces, these creatures suggest a dream's compression of images and the techniques of *Finnegans Wake*: the symbolic personification of lust in its mythical avatar and those fallen beings clothed in the shabby but soiled respectability of humanity suggest the animalism of sexuality and the shame frequently connected with the body. The *topoi* and motifs of this guilt-induced vision have been kindled by Father Arnall's fire and brimstone sermons, which, in turn, invoke centuries of Catholic imagery depicting the fates of the damned. Here, the content of dreams and visions calls on the collective unconscious of the Irish and western culture.

Joyce's later fiction represents a stylistic departure from these early visions. The cinematic creativity of Méliès has affinities with the apparitions and hallucinations of *Ulysses* and *Finnegans Wake*, which move toward a more fluid and transforming literature. The genre of the trick film may have provided Joyce with an apt model for his literary representations of dreams and fantasies.[2] A magician turned director, Méliès fully exploited the cinema's potential for illusion. As Gerald Mast explains, Méliès discerned "that the camera's ability to stop and start again brought the magician's two greatest arts to perfection—disappearance and conversion. Anything could be converted into anything else; anything could vanish" (38). The fluidity of change implicit here anticipates the nonlogical, free associational style favored by surrealism, creating a prototype of this art movement that, while closely yoked with the dream world, uses strikingly realistic images. Typical of this genre is Méliès's 1898 film *Un Homme de tête* (*Four Troublesome Heads*) in which the film maker portrays a magician who "removes his head three times over, strikes up a song with the resulting chorus, and then causes the extra heads to disappear by smashing them with a banjo" (Wakeman, 752). Or one might think of Billy Bitzer's *A Pipe Dream*, a 1905 Biograph production; the *Biograph Bulletin* provides the following synopsis of the company's trick film:

> A novel picture showing a young woman smoking a cigarette and dreamily blowing the smoke over the palm of her hand. As she watches the smoke the figure of a young man appears kneeling on her hand and addressing her in passionate terms. The image seems to amuse her greatly, and she tries to catch it. It vanishes as her hand goes to seize it. (Quoted in Barnouw, 100)

Whether apocryphal or not, Méliès's account of the discovery of the stop-motion effect has a resonance for readers of Joyce. Filming at the *Palace de l'Opéra*, the story goes, his camera jammed momentarily, resulting in a curious final product, according to the conjurer:

> During this minute, the passersby, buses, carriages had moved of course. When I projected the film, joined at the place where the break had occurred, I suddenly saw a Madeleine-Bastille bus changed into a hearse, and men changed into women. The substitution trick, called stop-motion, had been discovered. (Wakeman, 750)

Joyce would, as Lindsay prophesied of filmmakers, use such an effect in his cinematic prose, moving beyond simple tricks to more profound evocations. Lindsay suggested that "the possible charm in a so-called trick picture is in eliminating the tricks, giving them dignity till they are no longer such, but thoughts in motion and made visible" (142). The ease with which the passersby of Méliès moved between life and death and transformed from male to female suggests the types of transformations that Joyce so artfully employs in "Circe."

Much of *Ulysses*, especially "Circe" and the stream-of-consciousness passages, can be discussed using the terms which Lindsay employs to analyze the potential of the inchoate form—then often referred to as the photoplay—especially the type which he calls the "picture of Fairy Splendor." In the "Photoplay of Splendor," according to Lindsay, "the camera has a kind of Hallowe'en witch power" (59). This category includes a number of subcategories, including the picture of Fairy Splendor, by which he means the "highly imaginative fairy-tale" with its attendant trick scenes, those primitive forerunners to today's computer-generated special effects (62). With the motion-picture camera's ability to create sudden appearances and disappearances, transformations and other cinematic legerdemain, one can call up the dark spirits and macabre mood of Halloween and summon the type of supernatural and magical powers traditionally attributed to witches and warlocks. Lindsay might have been referring to films like Méliès's *Escamotage d'une dame chez Robert-Houdin* (*The Vanishing Lady*), in which not only does a woman disappear from a chair (as she did on stage at the Robert-Houdin theater), but also, with camera stops, he causes a skeleton to assume her place. Finally, the skeleton, too, disappears and the woman reappears seated in the chair. Or perhaps he had in mind a film such as *Le Diable géant, ou le miracle de la Madonne* (*The Devil and the Statue*), in which Satan, played by Méliès, "reaches giant proportions before a terrified Shakespearean Juliet and then, through the intercession of the Virgin Mary, shrinks to the size of a dwarf and disappears" (Wakeman, 750; 754). Such qualities and events have parallels both in the supernatural world of "Circe," in which images of Bloom's grandfather and son, as well as Stephen's mother, return from the grave, and in many of the macabre stream-of-consciousness passages that occur to Bloom in "Hades." Among a number of possibilities, consider the mental transformations of this passage regarding the caretaker of Glasvenin cemetery who, Bloom muses,

> has seen a fair share go under in his time, lying around him field after field. Holy fields. More room if they buried them standing. Sitting or kneeling you couldn't. Standing? His head might come up some day above ground in a landslip with his hand pointing. All honeycombed the ground must be: oblong cells. And very neat he keeps it too: trim grass and edgings. His garden Major Gamble calls Mount Jerome. Well, so it is. Ought to be flowers of sleep. Chinese cemeteries with giant poppies growing produce the best opium Mastiansky told me. The Botanic Gardens are just over there. It's the blood sinking in the earth gives new life. Same idea those jews they said killed the christian boy. Every man his price. Well preserved fat corpse, gentleman, epicure, invaluable for fruit garden. A bargain. By carcass of William Wilkinson, auditor and accountant, lately deceased, three pounds thirteen and six. With thanks. (6.763–75)

This chapter is, of course, particularly macabre because of its graveyard setting and Paddy Dignam's funeral, but the same grim sense and similar magical powers of combination and alteration can be found in other episodes. In "Lestrygonians," for example, Bloom ruminates upon some ideas of advertising campaigns for a former employer, Wisdom Hely, the stationer:

> I suggested . . . a transparent showcart with two smart girls sitting inside writing letters, copybooks, envelopes, blottingpaper. I bet that would have caught on. Smart girls writing something catch the eye at once. Everyone dying to know what she's writing. Get twenty of them round you if you stare at nothing. Have a finger in the pie. Women too. Curiosity. Pillar of salt. Wouldn't have it of course because he didn't think of it himself first. Or the inkbottle I suggested with a false stain of black celluloid. His ideas for ads like Plumtree's potted under the obituaries, cold meat department. (8.131–145)

Such grim collocations of curiosity that led to the gruesome saline death of Lot's wife alongside the horrific linkage of potted meat with corpses indicate the potentially macabre splicing of ideas made possible with a stream-of-consciousness that creates swift transmogrifications, with an apparent ease reminiscent of a stop-motion sequence in the cinema.

Similarly, magic transformations occur in connection with other topics than mortality and the fate of humans beyond and within the grave—a dairy woman and undergraduate life among them. In "Telemachus," for instance, the old dairy woman is subjected to the conversions imposed by a querulous Stephen who

> watched her pour into the measure and thence into the jug rich white milk, not hers. Old shrunken paps. She poured again a measureful and a tilly. Old and secret she had entered from a morning world, maybe a messenger. She praised the goodness of the milk, pouring it out. Crouching by a patient cow at daybreak in the lush field, a witch on her toadstool, her wrinkled fingers quick at the squirting dugs. They lowed about her whom they knew, dewsilky cattle. Silk of the kine and poor old woman, names given her in old times. A wandering crone, lowly form of an immortal serving her conqueror and her gay betrayer, their common cuckquean, a messenger from the secret morning. To serve or to upbraid, whether he could not tell: but scorned to beg her favour. (1.397–407)

The crone becomes the mother of Ireland, the queen of the fairies, the victim of imperialism and the female cuckold of the betraying Irish as she purveys her wares. Certainly, she is a likely candidate for alteration by the "Hallowe'en witch power" of the mind's screen and fits into the realm of fairy splendor. However, these changes summon not only mythical or traditional characters—a reference to an occurrence in Oxford brings up a vision, different in tone, yet similar in technique. Buck Mulligan remarks about Haines:

> If he makes any noise here I'll bring down Seymour and we'll give him a ragging worse than the one they gave Clive Kempthorpe.
>
> Young shouts of moneyed voices in Clive Kempthorpe's rooms. Palefaces: they hold their ribs with laughter, one clasping another. O, I shall expire! Break the news to her gently, Aubrey! I shall die! With slit ribbons of his shirt whipping the air he hops and hobbles round the table, with trousers down at heels, chased by Ades of Magdalen with the tailor's shears. A scared calf's face gilded with marmalade. I don't want to be debagged! Don't you play the giddy ox with me!
>
> Shouts from the open window startling evening in the quadrangle. A deaf gardener, aproned, masked with Matthew Arnold's

face, pushes his mower on the sombre lawn watching narrowly the dancing motes of grasshalms. (1.162–75)

Martello Tower thus becomes Magdalen college and a gardener assumes the face of that staunch defender of sweetness and light, Matthew Arnold. An Edwardian phantasm of an evening at Oxford is just as susceptible to magic conversion as a fairy vision from the Celtic twilight.

As Austin Briggs observes, this sorcerous power and its potentially horrifying emotional tenor manifests itself most obviously in the "Circe" episode. The stage directions of the episode indicate this from the outset:

> *(The Mabbot street entrance of nighttown, before which stretches an uncobbled tramsiding set with skeleton tracks, red and green will-o'-the-wisps and danger signals. Rows of grimy houses with gaping doors. Rare lamps with faint rainbow fans. Round Rabaiotti's halted ice gondola stunted men and women squabble. They grab wafers between which are wedged lumps of coral and copper snow. Sucking, they scatter slowly, children. The swancomb of the gondola, highreared, forges on through the murk, white and blue under a lighthouse. Whistles call and answer.)* (15.1–9)

The metaphoric skeletons, the stunted figures transforming into children, the danger and the darkness all contribute to the disturbing atmosphere. The whistles at first appear also to be a part of this squalid district of ill repute, however these sounds are seemingly embodied as The Call and The Answer who speak the first words of this hallucinatory drama.

A significant element of the visions in "Circe" can be linked to the type of animation that often occurs in the cinema, what Lindsay calls a "yearning for personality in furniture," an aspect that "begins to be crudely worked upon in the so-called trick scenes" (61). Lindsay mentions as a "typical ... comedy of this sort" a film titled "Moving Day," in which the furniture and possessions of a household march by themselves from one domicile to another, relocating the family in short order. He might also have mentioned an early Dewar's Whiskey advertisement of Méliès: during the film, the solemn "family portraits descend from their frames to sample" the scotch being served (Barnouw, 101). Other later examples include Oscar Fischinger's animated advertisements during the 1930's, some of which featured armies of marching Muratti cigarettes. Similarly, inanimate objects are imbued with personality, including the power of speech, in the Circean psychodrama. The legion of furnishings, animals, elements and even actions which (or who) exhibit personality range from the Wreaths of cigarette smoke to the Kisses for Bloom, from the bleats of Staggering Bob, "a whitepolled calf" to the "bright cascade" of the Poulaphouca Waterfall of the upper Liffey—named, quite appropriately, after the Celtic version of the sprite Puck, Phouka (Gifford, 15.3299). Each is given voice and identity by the stage directions and dialogue in the episode, the calf and the waterfall possibly having been witnesses to a masturbatory indiscretion of the young Leopold Bloom. (Perhaps, they saw; evidence in "Circe" can hardly be relied upon.)

While these apparitions may surprise the reader, comments in earlier episodes prefigure them. In "Lestrygonians," Mrs. Breen tells Bloom of her husband Denis's nightmare in which "the ace of spades was walking up the stairs" (8.253). And both Stephen and Bloom remark upon the often ignored voices of the inanimate world: in "Proteus," the young poet/aesthete listens to "a fourworded wavespeech: seesoo, hrss, rsseeiss, ooos. Vehement breath of waters amid seasnakes, rearing horses, rocks. In cups of rocks it slops: flop, slop, slap: bounded in barrels. And, spent, its speech ceases. It flows purling, widely lowing, floating, foampool, flower unfurling" (3.456–60). The more practical Bloom notes in "Aeolus" that machines and objects speak:

> Sllt. The nethermost deck of the first machine jogged forward its flyboard with sllt the first batch of quirefolded papers. Sllt. Almost human the way it sllt to call attention. Doing its level best to speak. That door too still creaking, asking to be shut. Everything speaks in its own way. Sllt. (7.174–177)

Each of these passages is more than the onomatopoeia of Joyce's earlier work, like the sound of the cricket bats in *Portrait*: "pick, pack, pock, puck"; they represent nonhuman speech as interpreted by these two observers, individuals who attempt to discern the personality of the world about them, depicted by an author who, like the cinematic magician, animates lifeless objects.

Lindsay also suggests that in "all photoplays . . . human beings tend to become dolls and mechanisms, and dolls and mechanisms tend to become human" (53). He anticipates what Bazin would later consider the cinema's "specific illusion ": "to make of a revolver or of a face the very center of the universe" (1: 105). One of the most human aspects of mechanisms in Joyce's work—speech—has already been discussed. However, in many of the episodes of *Ulysses*, Joyce also imbues humans with apparently mechanical qualities: reminding one of the machine-like antics of silent film stars such as Max Linder, Charlie Chaplin or Harold Lloyd. The characters in "Wandering Rocks" resemble automatons, comprising the moving parts of a Dublin machine; in "Sirens," the humans are frequently reduced to brief musical equivalents; while in "Oxen of the Sun," Bloom, Stephen and the medical students all find themselves subjected to the ventriloquism of the author's gestational/literary-historical obsession; finally, in "Circe," Bloom's stiff-walk turns his movements into mechanical ones.[3]

But perhaps more importantly, Joyce does attain the potential that Lindsay foresees in the photoplay of fairy splendor, "the possible charm in a so-called trick picture," by recreating "thoughts in motion," literally embodying ideas and emotions (142). "Circe" represents the character's consciousness in motion, rendering the ideas and emotions of Stephen and Bloom apparent to the reader, not through the usual novelistic means of description or even by entering their stream-of-consciousness, a device readers of Joyce have become quite accustomed to much earlier in the novel.[4] Fantasies and thoughts are given shape and substance; the mind is projected, but as dreamlike representations rather than through means like the disproportion described in Chapter IV. For example, Bloom's trial for a catalogue of numerous and varied sex crimes—a fantasy which starts shortly after he finds himself confronted with this graffiti in nighttown: "*a scrawled chalk legend* Wet Dream *and a phallic design*" (15.649–50)—objectifies and projects his most secret desires baldly for all readers to see and hear, to follow unequivocally, while at the same time demonstrating his own guilt concerning these longings. The apparition of Shakespeare as cuckold is similarly evocative of many buried themes:

LYNCH

(*points*) The mirror up to nature. (*he laughs*) Hu hu hu hu hu!

(*Stephen and Bloom gaze in the mirror. The face of William Shakespeare, beardless, appears there, rigid in facial paralysis, crowned by the reflection of the reindeer antlered hatrack in the hall.*)

SHAKESPEARE

(*in dignified ventriloquy*) 'Tis the loud laugh bespeaks the vacant mind. (*to Bloom*) Thou thoughtest as how thou wastest invisible.

Gaze. (*he crows with a black capon's laugh*) Iagogo! How my Oldfellow chokit his Thursdaymornun. Iagogogo!

BLOOM

(*smiles yellowly at the three whores*) When will I hear the joke? (15.3820–31)

Through the logic of dreams and the unconscious, one finds here a cinematic representation of issues and themes related to important motifs in the novel. With his allusion, one of those "chance words" that evoke memories—as "Oxen of the Sun" describes them (14.1348)—Lynch calls forth the bard and the question of artistic creation (see below). Shakespeare first mouths words that are actually a variation of Oliver Goldsmith's *The Deserted Village*, raising the issue of artistry and plagiarism. Yet before Shakespeare even speaks, his appearance as antlered cuckold in the mirror brings to mind the displacement of both Bloom and Stephen. Like Bloom, Stephen has of course been denied by a usurper, although not to the joys of the marriage bed at 7 Eccles Street, but of access to his castle-home in Sandymount. Furthermore, the vision of Shakespeare taunts Bloom with the hope that his transgressions would not be found out and derides him with the laughter of a black (hence ostracized like the Moor) castrated rooster. Bloom doubts his own masculinity through this apparition, who further mocks him with the punning variations of Othello and Desdemona—Oldfellow and Thursdaymornun—reminding him both of the waning of sexual prowess generally expected with middle age and the morning when he said nothing ("chokit") to prevent the adulterous liaison of his wife. With this densely layered passage, foreshadowing both the themes and the sort of encoding ubiquitous in *Finnegans Wake*, we certainly have moved beyond the tricks of the cinema to the dignity and artistry of thoughts in motion.

Certainly this passage and others like it suggest, as Lindsay comments, "how much more quickly than on the stage the borderline of All Saints' Day and Hallowe'en can be crossed. Note how easily memories are called up, and appear in the midst of the room. In any [photo-]plays whatever, you will find these apparitions and recollections. . . . The dullest hero is given glorious visualizing power" (65–66). In his chapter "Furniture, Trappings, and Inventions in Motion," Lindsay provides a lengthy summary and analysis of a Griffith film, *The Avenging Conscience*, a collage of macabre scenes in homage to and in imitation of Edgar Allan Poe. In this film, Griffith effortlessly enters the world of dreams and horror, giving the audience filmic access to the mind of the tale's protagonist/poet and allowing them to experience the frightening rearrangements of his daily life into nightmares of murder and persecution. Likewise, using cinematic means, Joyce can easily take the reader into the depths of Bloom's and Stephen's personal Halloweens, their particular houses of horrors. We traverse the boundaries between saints and sinners, moving from All Hallow's Eve to All Saints' Day quite readily; in "Circe," the Voice of All the Blessed follows hard on the Voice of All the Damned—the difference between "the Lord God Omnipotent" and "Tnetopinmo Dog Drol eht" (as the chorus of the damned renders His name backwards) is only six short lines (see 15.4700–720). As Lindsay suggests may occur in film, memories are called up throughout *Ulysses*—as noted above, a passage from "Oxen of the Sun" explains the explosion of repressed occurrences and secret reflections in "Circe." In the voice of Cardinal Newman, the book informs us:

> There are sins or (let us call them as the world calls them) evil memories which are hidden away by man in the darkest places of the heart but they abide there and wait. He may suffer their memory to grow dim, let them be as though they had not been and all but persuade himself that they were not or at least were otherwise. Yet a chance word will call them forth suddenly and they will rise up to confront him in the most various circumstances, a vision or a dream, or while timbrel and harp soothe his senses or amid the cool silver tranquility of the evening or at the feast, at midnight, when he is now filled with wine. (14.1344–1355)

A "chance word" may evoke memories in "Circe," but such stimuli also bring up memories in other episodes: in "Calypso," reminiscences of earlier life with Molly arise; in "Proteus," Stephen remembers the Paris of Kevin Egan; and in "Nestor," Sargent, Stephen's student, triggers recollections of his own school days at Clongowes. Through Joyce's tricks that parallel those of the cinema, Bloom, our dullest hero, is given glorious, if sometimes frightening, visualizing power in many episodes of the novel, but especially in the phantasmagoria of "Circe."

In fact, "Circe" represents a stunning departure from what we expect of a novel; not much more than a generation ago even such an astute critic as Vladimir Nabokov could comment, "I do not know of any commentator who has correctly understood this chapter" (350). Due to its unusual qualities, critics often search for literary precedents. The list of sources that they generally offer as potential models for "Circe" includes the *Walpurgisnacht* section of Goethe's *Faust*, Flaubert's *The Temptation of St. Anthony*, and Strindberg's *A Dream Play*. Yet the common element between these works seems to be their use of words and descriptions to create the type of illusions readily achievable by the magic of the cinema. If trick films did not actually inspire Joyce, at the very least he borrowed literary techniques from earlier attempts at what could be considered a cinematic form.

The form, tone and technique of the episode can certainly be traced to these sources that Joyce undoubtedly knew. Goethe's *Walpurgisnacht*, that magic-filled and demonic orgy of spring, with its talking will-o'-the-wisp, its choruses of witches and wizards and its disembodied voices, clearly offers one precedent and influences the nightmarish tone of the episode. Flaubert's *The Temptation of St. Anthony* provided a model for both the content and the appearance of "Circe," as one can discern from this excerpt:

> And now, across the whole basilica, redoubled frenzy breaks out.
>
> The Audians shoot arrows at the Devil; the Collyridians toss blue veils up to the ceiling; the Ascites bow down before a wineskin; the Marcionites baptise a dead man with oil. Next to Apelles a woman, the better to explain her idea, exhibits a round loaf in a bottle; another in the middle of the Sampsenes distributes, as if it were the host, the dust from her sandals. On the Marcosian's rose-strewn bed two lovers embrace. The Circumcellions cut each other's throats, the Valesians lie gasping, Bardesanes chants, Caprocrates dances, Maximilla and Priscilla moan resoundingly—and the false prophetess of Cappadocia, quite naked, resting her elbows on a lion and waving three torches, howls the Terrible Invocation.
>
> The columns sway like tree-trunks, the amulets round the heretics' necks criss-cross in fiery lines, the constellations in the chapels quiver, and the walls give way to the coming and going of the crowd, whose every head is a wave which leaps and roars.
>
> But then—from the very heart of the uproar, with bursts of laughter—a song rises in which the name of Jesus recurs.
>
> These are plebeian folk, all beating their hands to mark time. In the middle of them is

ARIUS

in deacon's costume.

> *The fools who rail against me claim to explain the absurd; and to leave them quite at a loss I've composed some little poems, so funny that people know them off by heart in the mills and the taverns and the ports.*

> *A thousand times no! The Son is not co-eternal with the Father, nor of the same substance!* (116–17)

The crowded hallucinations, though peopled with folk from the ancient ecclesiastical world rather than Edwardian Dubliners, the layout incorporating various typographical devices to indicate the action and description of the hallucinations, and the magic of a scene in which a building and its decorations sway, while the heads of the crowd become waves—all these qualities predict the form and substance of "Circe" and could only be visually represented and convincingly depicted in film.[5]

However, Strindberg's *A Dream Play* may be the most important source for "Circe." In a preface to this work, the author defines this new genre: in it, the author attempts

> to imitate the inconsequent yet transparently logical shape of a dream. Everything can happen, everything is possible and probable. Time and place do not exist; on an insignificant basis of reality, the imagination spins, weaving new patterns; a mixture of memories, experiences, free fancies, incongruities and improvisations. The characters split, double, multiply, evaporate, condense, disperse, assemble. But one consciousness rules over them all, that of the dreamer, for him there are no secrets, no illogicalities, no scruples, no laws. He neither acquits nor condemns, but merely relates; and just as a dream is often more painful than happy, so an undertone of melancholy and of pity for all mortal beings accompanies this *flickering tale*. (175, emphasis added)

Even the set of *A Dream Play* could only be mimetically represented through the magic of cinematic special effects. Within three pages, and without a pause for the substitution of props nor time to allow for the striking of the set, a lime-tree transforms from the barrenness of autumn to the green of spring again and the nearly withered monk's-hood blossoms anew (196–98). The audience of the play might suspend their disbelief and accept a change of lighting to represent the seasonal transformations, but to follow the stage directions *literally*, to relate such a "flickering tale," would require the magic of the movies.[6]

Joyce himself realized the connection between "Circe" and the cinema; if unaware of the affinity at the time of composition, it certainly became clear to him later. As noted earlier, in the "Circe" section of his notebook for *Finnegans Wake*, *Scribbledehobble*, he writes: "Cinema fakes, drown, state of sea, tank, steeplejack, steeple on floor, camera above; jumps 10 feet, 1 foot camera in 6 foot pit" (119). The notebook entry itself suggests a staged drowning, in a tank made to look like the sea. A crewman perches on a steeple with the camera above aiming down; it may look as though an actor jumps 10 feet, but it is probably just a camera in a deeper hole that creates the illusion. Such an entry not only demonstrates Joyce's awareness of cinema tricks, but also that he believed film to be related to "Circe" in the context of the workbook and the technique of the episode. It also implies the relationship of the movies to *Finnegans Wake*, a work in which the magic is even more complex, the changes quicker. Complex meanings emerge in a multilayered fashion from a single word or phrase from the *Wake*; at the level of a scene or a speech from the work, ambiguities and possible interpretations run nearly rampant. Tricks abound and Joyce uses them to tell the recurring stories of the human fall and the cycles of history told and retold in *Finnegans Wake*—but a complete examination of the relationship between Joyce's last complex work and the cinema is a subject for future study. These hints and the notebook's explicit connection with "Circe," however, further strengthen the case that Joyce's interest in the cinema was far from an idle pastime: with its technical wizardry, movies represent an ideal model for a literary means to recreate the dreams and fancies of Leopold Bloom and Stephen Dedalus, as well as those multiply-exposed visions seen by the sleeping Humphrey Chimpden Earwicker and related to us by the narrator of the *Wake*. The illusions of the trick film also share affinities with the personalized but inanimate world of "Aeolus," the psychological drama of "Circe" and the streams-of-consciousness which Joyce presents to the reader throughout *Ulysses*.

NOTES

[1] Austin Briggs first pointed out the connection between Lindsay and "Circe" in a paper delivered at the Copenhagen Joyce symposium, subsequently published in *Coping with Joyce*; see the list of works cited.

[2] According to Robert Ryf, Georges Méliès exhibited his films near Joyce's residence in Paris in 1904 (see Ch. 1, Note 2); he is also the most

famous of the many early *cineastes* who had roots in the world of magic. See Erik Barnouw's *The Magician and the Cinema*.

[3]Mary Parr, in her study, *James Joyce: The Poetry of Conscience, A Study of* Ulysses, links Chaplin to Bloom's stiff-walk in "Circe."

[4]Whether, as Vladimir Nabokov and others have maintained, "Circe" represents *Ulysses* itself dreaming, the thoughts are still motivated—literally moved, as its etymology suggests.

[5]In the winter of 1898–99, Méliès filmed a version of *The Temptation of St. Anthony*, suggesting the cinematic magic inherent in the story. In his version, he utilizes the tricks of the camera to create a scene which Joyce certainly would have appreciated: "the camera-stop is used to transform a statue of Christ on the cross into a seductive woman" (Wakeman, 752).

[6]Certainly, one could follow the stagecraft of the absurdist theater to enact such scenes, as Victoria Shaskan, one of my students, has suggested to me. However, such devices would only convey the affect of the changes and not their appearances.

CHAPTER SIX
A Look Between
A Cinematic Analysis of "Nausicaa"

> Pity they can't see themselves.
> —*Ulysses* 13.792-93

> She saw that he saw.
> —*Ulysses* 13.726

The "Nausicaa" episode of *Ulysses* is one of the most cinematically compelling pieces of Joyce's work. Moreover, Bloom's voyeurism, Gerty's coquetry and the episode's vivid description make "Nausicaa" particularly well-suited to analysis through feminist film theory. A major focus of feminist film theory involves the concept of identification between the spectator and the characters of the classical narrative film. Janet Bergstrom suggests the range of identifications: "it is now possible and absolutely necessary to complicate the question of identification as it functions in the classical film, first of all in terms of the realization that spectators are able to take up multiple identificatory positions, whether successively or simultaneously" (181–2). Acknowledging the complexity of this topic, I intend to limit this chapter to only two of the multifarious spectator identifications within "Nausicaa." First, I will draw upon Laura Mulvey's important essay on male and female roles within classical cinema, "Visual Pleasure and Narrative Cinema" (a piece which Tania Modleski suggests "may be considered the founding document of psychoanalytic feminist film theory") to analyze the response of the male reader/spectator to the episode (1). Then, utilizing two of Mary Ann Doane's essays on female spectatorship, "*Caught* and *Rebecca*: The Inscription of Femininity as Absence" and "Film and the Masquerade: Theorising the Female Spectator," I will address the female reader/spectator's reaction to "Nausicaa." I will also consider the roles of both Bloom and Gerty as spectators within the novel.[1]

In "Visual Pleasure and Narrative Cinema," Laura Mulvey argues that "mainstream film coded the erotic into the language of the dominant patriarchal order" (59). She maintains that the pleasures of looking in the classical narrative cinema are two: "the first, scopophilic, arises from the pleasure in using another person as an object of sexual stimulation through sight. The second, developed through narcissism and the constitution of the ego, comes from identification with the [male] image seen" (61). Moreover, in this cinema, the male tends to be active and controlling within a mirrored reality (59), while the female appears unrealistically iconic and passive, destroying the "illusion of depth demanded by the narrative," having "the quality of a cut-out" (63). This portrayal of females gives the males within the narrative and all spectators (but particularly men, I would argue) the masculinized power of looking, which usually manifests itself in one of two ways: voyeurism—"investigating the woman, demystifying her mystery"—or fetishistic scopophilia, which "builds up the physical beauty of the object, transforming it into something satisfying in itself" (64). The cinema, by dictating what we see and how we see it, influences our perception and reinforces stereotyped roles of men and women. As Mulvey suggests: "None of these interacting layers is intrinsic to film, but it is only in the film form that they can reach a perfect and beautiful contradiction, thanks to the possibility in the cinema of shifting the emphasis of the look. It is the place of the look that defines cinema, the possibility of varying it and exposing it" (67). Clearly *Ulysses*, a novel concerned with parallax and recounting the odyssey of a voyeuristic male protagonist, also possesses many of these qualities.

In addition to the active/passive dichotomy, Mulvey points to a "heterosexual division of labor" which "has similarly controlled narrative structure. . . . [T]he split between spectacle and narrative supports the man's role as the active one of forwarding the story, making things happen" (63). "Nausicaa," an episode dominated by erotic spectacle, certainly follows another that epitomizes the concept of the "active" male "making things happen": "Cyclops." The gathering of men at Barney Kiernan's pub, which leads to one of the few violent acts in the novel, is quickly followed by an idyllic interlude, a rendering of daylight's waning and the evocation of the iconic Gerty. The portrayal of the male world of action ends with a ballistic simile— "like a shot off a shovel" (12.1918)—as the depiction of the female sphere begins with a conventional personification of the soft twilight: "The summer evening had begun to fold the world in its mysterious embrace" (13.1–2). Even the feminized hour is to be looked upon in its mystery: likewise, the spiritual succor of Mary, star of the sea, ought to be regarded as "pure radiance [,] a beacon ever to the stormtossed heart of man," that active participant (13.7–8)—here, of course, being Bloom escaped from the Citizen's wrath, resting after the trip to the Widow Dignam's and avoiding an early and disruptive arrival at home.

These narrative strands are interrupted by the spectacle that is Gerty, being watched by Bloom, the narrator and, by proxy, the male readers.[2] For, "as the spectator identifies with the main male protagonist, he projects his look onto that of his like, his screen surrogate, so that the power of the male protagonist as he controls events coincides with the active power of the erotic look, both giving a satisfying sense of omnipotence" (Mulvey 63). Thus, the male reader closely identifies with Bloom; and Bloom's interpretation of events tends to shape the reader's impression of the novel's women, especially Gerty.

If we accept Mulvey's orthodox Freudian view (with its implicit Lacanian tinge), then the man must have a mechanism that controls the castration anxiety of which the woman remains a symbol. Such mastery is important for the man to maintain his traditional power, and he performs certain actions in order to retain that patriarchal hold. In "Nausicaa," Bloom is particularly sensitive to the threat of women, since his stopped watch pointedly reminds him of Molly's assignation with Boylan. Bloom acknowledges, at some level, that his wife's adultery represents a blow to his manhood, a temporary castration, if you will. His bold observation of Gerty suggests his attempt to regain the control over women that Molly's infidelity has appropriated.

Mulvey explains the power of the male gaze as a means of controlling women:

> The male unconscious has two avenues of escape from this castration anxiety: preoccupation with the re-enactment of the original trauma (investigating the woman, demystifying her mystery), . . . or else complete disavowal of castration by the substitution of a fetish object or turning the represented figure itself into a fetish so

that it becomes reassuring rather than dangerous (hence overvaluation, the cult of the female star). (64)

The alternatives, then, are voyeurism and scopophilia.

Scopophilia, making an object into a visualized fetish (to utilize Mulvey's vocabulary), is the more obvious attempt to control women and the anxiety they create. In *Ulysses*, and in "Nausicaa" in particular, as with film, "the determining male gaze projects its phantasy on to the female figure which is styled accordingly" (62). Furthermore, Mulvey maintains that "in their traditional exhibitionist role women are simultaneously looked at and displayed, with their appearance coded for strong visual and erotic impact so that they can be said to connote *to-be-looked-at-ness*" (62). Scopophilia can be glimpsed in nearly all of the episodes in which Bloom appears. The female characters are frequently reduced to "one part of a fragmented body," objectified by the males (62). In "Lotus-Eaters," for example, Bloom partakes in a long and ultimately frustrating act of scopophilic indulgence. Watching for the "silk flash rich stockings white" of a lady "proud: rich," as he engages in perfunctory conversation with M'Coy, Bloom finds himself thwarted by "a heavy tramcar" slewing between his lascivious gaze and the object of his prurient interest (5.120, 130–31). The action, i.e., the conversation, is interrupted (indeed intercut) by his glances, as Mulvey suggests often occurs: "the presence of woman" freezes "the flow of action in moments of erotic contemplation" (62). Similarly, in "Eumaeus," the "fleshy charms" of Molly are desired and possessed by the eyes of both Stephen and Bloom, the males in the novel, as well as those reading the novel:

> Stephen, obviously addressed, looked down on the photo showing a large sized lady with her fleshy charms on evidence in an open fashion as she was in the full bloom [note the possessive pun] of womanhood in evening dress cut ostentatiously low for the occasion to give a liberal display of bosom, with more than vision of breasts, her full lips parted and some perfect teeth, standing near, ostensibly with gravity, a piano on the rest of which was *In Old Madrid*, a ballad, pretty in its way, which was then all the vogue. Her (the lady's) eyes, dark, large, looked at Stephen, about to smile about something to be admired, Lafayette of Westmoreland street, Dublin's premier photographic artist, being responsible for the esthetic execution. (16.1427–1436)

The possession by Stephen, the erotic contemplation, the anticipation of that still and frozen moment—photography and its prolonged gaze creating the perfect opportunity for objectification (and ultimately, frighteningly, a form of "execution")—all indicate the iconic female in relation to the male characters and spectators.

In "Nausicaa," the relationship between the sexes occupies most of the chapter and the fetishization of women is clearly demonstrated throughout the episode with many women: from the "typist going up Roger Greene's stairs two at a time to show her understandings" to the desire for "a full length oilpainting of" Molly as she looked when she and Bloom were courting (13.916–19 and 1091–1092). In the first few pages, however, it is Gerty who is described by the narrator and observed by the reader, and by Bloom, as a series of beautiful fragments. In many ways, Gerty clearly resembles a "cut-out" from "women's" magazines—she represents an icon of that ilk (albeit flawed by fate), while also being the product of hints from "those shiny columns of advice," as Sandra Gilbert describes them in her sonnet to a descendant of the *Princess Novelette*, and the *Lady's Pictorial*: the *Ladies' Home Journal*.

The episode's focus, "in very truth, as fair a specimen of winsome Irish girlhood as one could wish to see," is slowly examined in answer to that incisive question of identity: "But who was Gerty?" She is clearly a combination of a "slight and graceful" figure, a face of "waxen pallor . . . almost spiritual in its ivorylike purity though her rosebud mouth was a genuine Cupid's bow," with "eyes of witchery," crowned by "a wealth of wonderful hair . . . dark brown with a natural wave in it," recently trimmed "on account of the new moon" (13.78–122). Joyce provides us with a full description of Gerty, halting all action on the beach to allow narrator and male reader alike to linger over her image, examining its components lovingly, like a camera panning over the female star upon her first entrance—for example, Lana Turner's appearance in *The Postman Always Rings Twice*, or Lauren Bacall in *To Have and Have Not*. In the description of our Nausicaa, and certainly later in the chapter's famous fireworks scene, Gerty fits Mulvey's analysis: "Woman displayed as sexual object is the leit-motif of erotic spectacle: . . . she holds the look, plays to and signifies male desire" (62). The fetishization of the female is thus accomplished by the narrator and the male reader simultaneously, as they look upon the fragmentation of Gerty.

Yet, in this episode, Joyce has gone beyond the scopophilic—woman becomes more than a fetish. Gerty is, in fact, also subjected to that voyeuristic demystification that Mulvey discusses. There is an attempt by the narrator and the male reader to enter the "female" world of romance. That first description of Gerty discussed above is, of course, interwoven with commentary about the methods by which she achieves certain tantalizing effects. The mysterious secrets of her beauty are revealed by the narrator: a figure saved from fragility by "iron jelloids," hands "as white as lemonjuice and queen of ointments could make them," eyes enhanced by the advice of "Madame Vera Verity, directress of the Woman Beautiful page of the Princess Novelette," and a torso covered by "a neat blouse of electric blue selftinted by dolly dyes (because it was expected in the *Lady's Pictorial* that electric blue would be worn)" (13.84–151).

Bloom, the narrator and the male reader alike are entranced by Gerty's loveliness. All gaze at her intently, passionately, seldom looking away. The power of the male gaze is confirmed when Bloom ejaculates—his imaginary possession of Gerty is complete (if temporary), and man's traditional control over woman has been asserted (although from a distance). In Bloom's portion of the episode, he recognizes that Gerty's carefully constructed appearance was meant to entice: "Dressed up to the nines for somebody. Fashion part of their charm. . . . Out on spec probably" (13.804–08). He also acknowledges the artificiality and staged quality of the situation, "see her as she is spoil all. Must have the stage setting, the rouge, costume, position, music. . . . Curtain up. . . . Maiden discovered with pensive bosom" (13.855–58). Nevertheless, on one level, Bloom's purported male superiority has been reestablished—"the strength it gives a man" (13.859).

On a more sinister note, while a woman's stylishness is undeniably appealing to such a man, it also lures his attention away from the "masculine" world, and is therefore menacing. The power of the male gaze, even when brought to a satisfactory conclusion as in "Nausicaa," evidently cannot remove this threat completely. Although Bloom obviously enjoyed looking at Gerty, he feels hostile toward her, cursing her for causing him to succumb to her charms (which leads to a transitory lack of masculinity): "Drained all the manhood out of me, little wretch" (13.1101–02). In Bloom's mind, Gerty is a villain who has harmed him. After their sexual encounter, he seems to compare her to a murderer, considering himself her weak (but willing) victim: "O! Exhausted that female has me. Not so young now. Will she come here tomorrow? Wait for her somewhere for ever. Must come back. Murderers do. Will I?" (13.1253–55).

His assessment of the experience with Gerty is markedly uncharitable. One might expect Bloom to consider the titillation an isolated, exhilarating incident and to muse benevolently about Gerty's character and situation. Instead, he makes crude generalizations about the sexual craving of women: "Yours for the asking. Because they want it themselves. Their natural craving. . . . Don't want it they throw it at you" (13.790–92). The following passage, however, suggests a source for some of Bloom's beliefs: "Pity they can't see themselves. A dream of well-filled hose. Where was that? Ah, yes. Mutoscope pictures in Capel street: for men only. Peeping Tom. Willy's hat and what the girls did with it. Do they snapshot those girls or is it all a fake? *Lingerie* does it. Felt for the curves inside her *deshabille*" (13.792–96). They do indeed "snapshot those girls" in the process of producing a mutoscopic show and one of the presentations he recalls—that "dream of well-filled hose"—achieves the fragmentation of women in a graphic and, due to the persistence of vision, animated form.[3]

According to the citations quoted in the *Oxford English Dictionary*, the mutoscope itself inspired a certain moral outrage. The *Westminster Gazette* notes in 1899: "the impression that we have been indulging in a mutoscopic debauch." In 1902, a member of Parliament, Samuel Smith decries "not only . . . the open and shameless exhibition of vice in the streets and low theatres but . . . [also] the vile papers, pictures and mutoscopic exhibitions which corrupted the young wholesale" (464). Such furor at animating pornographic images with early film devices might well be compared to that generated by pornographic software in which the user controls the actions of the female image.

Furthermore, the regret initially expressed—"Pity they can't see themselves"—and the reference to the eponymous "Peeping Tom" underscore how the perspective of the male spectator is represented in *Ulysses* and dominates cinematic presentation and narrative grammar, as Mulvey suggests in her later essay "Afterthoughts on 'Visual Pleasure and Narrative Cinema' inspired by *Duel in the Sun*."

As Bloom enjoys his post-masturbatory nap, fetishization, female images and pornography all become part of his dreams. He recreates, indeed stylizes, his memory of the scene on the beach—combining his reflections upon Gerty's actions, Molly's recent and distant past, Martha's letter and refrains from *Sweets of Sin*:

> O sweety all your little girlwhite up I saw dirty bracegirdle made me do love sticky we two naughty Grace darling she him half past the bed met him pike hoses frillies for Raoul de perfume your wife black hair heave under embon *señorita* young eyes Mulvey plump bubs me breadvan Winkle red slippers she rusty sleep wander years of dreams return tail end Agendath swoony lovey showed me her next year in drawers return next in her next her next. (13.1279-85)

He reorders and replays them, in a scopophilic montage of memories, fantasies and dreams—that "most heroic attempt" at a "full embrace of the whole inner world" for which Eisenstein praised Joyce (184). He creates the composite woman, "thereby producing an illusion cut to the measure of desire" (Mulvey, 67).

Thus one can analyze the male responses to Gerty: those of a character and the reader/spectator. But how does Gerty regard herself and what options for identification are there for the female reader? A persistent query to Mulvey after the publication of "Narrative Cinema and Visual Pleasure" was "what about the women in the audience?"("Afterthoughts," 69). In an attempt to construct "a female spectator," Mary Ann Doane analyzes two of Hollywood's quintessential "woman's pictures" from the forties in her article "*Caught* and *Rebecca*: The Inscription of Femininity as Absence." It may be helpful to regard "Nausicaa" as the "woman's" episode of *Ulysses*, for the moment, allowing us to examine the chapter utilizing certain aspects of Doane's analyses. In a subsequent article, "Film and the Masquerade: Theorising the Female Spectator," Doane elaborates upon the ideas introduced in her earlier piece. Both essays and other work on the masquerade provide insight into Gerty and the female spectator.

In her article on *Caught* and *Rebecca*, Doane maintains that "'women's films' are based on an idea of female fantasy which they [women] themselves anticipate and in some sense construct. . . . The films manifest an obsession with certain psychical mechanisms which have been associated with the female." In this light, Gerty's portion of the chapter may be regarded as an analogue to these films. Her obsession takes the form of the romantic daydreaming typically attributed to young women. In the beginning of Gerty's portion, we learn that she has created an elaborate, detailed fantasy of courtship and marriage with Reggy Wylie and longs to see him that evening. Her hopes are buoyed by romantic superstition: "she thought perhaps he might be out because when she was dressing that morning she nearly slipped up the old pair on her inside out and that was for luck and lovers' meeting if you put those things on inside out or if they got untied that he was thinking about you so long as it wasn't of a Friday" (13.183–7).

As the episode progresses, Gerty's romantic thoughts shift from Reggy to an imaginary suitor and husband. Gerty has, with her conventional fancy, even prophesied the character and appearance of the future man in her life:

> he who would woo and win Gerty MacDowell must be a man among men. . . . No prince charming is her beau ideal to lay a rare and wondrous love at her feet but rather a manly man with a strong quiet face who had not found his ideal, perhaps his hair slightly flecked with grey, and who would understand, take her in his sheltering arms, strain her to him in all the strength of his deep passionate nature and comfort her with a long long kiss. It would be like heaven. (13.206–214)

Her prognostications surpass the description of her dreamhusband; she proceeds to envision their domestic bliss with a wealth of detail, including their "creature comforts . . . griddlecakes done to a goldenbrown hue . . . a beautifully appointed drawingroom with pictures and engravings and . . . that silver toastrack in Clery's summer jumble sales" (13.222–242). Finally, Gerty notices the anonymous man on the beach whom we know as Leopold Bloom: "Here was that of which she had so often dreamed. It was he who mattered and there was joy on her face because she wanted him because she felt instinctively that he was like no-one else. The very heart of the girlwoman went out to him, her dreamhusband, because she knew on the instant it was him" (13.427–31). To Gerty, Bloom represents the potential fulfillment of all of her dreams.

In her longing to realize her romantic fantasies, Gerty has taken great care to make herself attractive. She anticipates what men yearn for and constructs her image in that manner, according to her guidebooks, those "women's" magazines:

> Gerty was dressed simply but with the instinctive taste of a votary of Dame Fashion for she felt there was just a might that he might be out. A neat blouse . . . with a smart vee opening down to the division and kerchief pocket (in which she always kept a piece of cottonwool scented with her favourite perfume because the handkerchief spoiled the sit) and a navy threequarter skirt cut to the

stride showed off her slim graceful figure to perfection. (13.148–155)

Gerty has studied her lessons so well that this desire to appeal to men has become "instinctive" within her. She dresses to hold the male look, as her shirtwaist and skirt indicate: her cleavage, euphemistically called "the division," slightly exposed and a slit skirt to display "just the proper amount and no more of her shapely limbs encased in fingerspun hose" (13. 169–70). Not even a handkerchief is allowed to spoil the contour of her blouse. In later work Doane will adopt Joan Riviere's term "masquerade" to describe woman's constructed image (see below) and, as Stephen Heath suggests, "the masquerade is the woman's thing, hers, but is also exactly *for* the man, a male presentation, as he would have her" (50).

But how does the female reader/spectator view Gerty? Because a "woman's" film tells a story from the female protagonist's point of view, it "offers resistance to an analysis which stresses the 'to-be-looked-at-ness' of the woman, her objectification as spectacle according to the masculine structure of the gaze. . . . One assumption behind the positing of a female spectator (that is, one who does not assume a masculine position with respect to the reflected image of her own body) is that it is no longer necessary to invest the look with desire in quite the same way" (Doane, 197). To appeal to a woman spectator then, the image of woman in a film, or, in this case, a novel, must play upon the female spectator's need to be desirable to men (Doane, 198). In reading Gerty's portion of "Nausicaa," if Doane is correct, a woman may very well wish that the admiring language used by the narrator to describe Gerty could also be applied to her, or that she had the time and energy not only to peruse articles on beauty and fashion, but also to purchase and apply the items supposedly necessary to achieve the advertised results.

The portrayal of the female protagonist reinforces the woman spectator's need to be desirable by showing the protagonist's preoccupation with her appearance. As Doane suggests, "the desire of the woman [as represented in these exempla of 'women's' films] is to duplicate a given image, to engage with and capture the male gaze" (198). Gerty herself has become a consumer subject to the dictates of fashion and trend. With her preoccupation with *accoutrements* and millinery, her commitment as a "votary of Dame Fashion," Gerty resembles these women (13.148–49). She is an ancestor of Leonora of Max Ophüls's *Caught*, whose statements of desire "are the indexical actualizations of the female appetite for the image, an appetite sustained by the commodity fetishism which supports capitalism. And the ultimate commodity . . . is the body adorned for the gaze" (198). As noted earlier, Bloom recognizes by her stylishness that Gerty seeks to draw attention to herself. He suspects that fashion, rather than the woman herself, may be the primary source of a woman's allure: "Say a woman loses a charm with every pin she takes out" (13.802–03). And, underscoring the commercial aspect of it all, he theorizes about Gerty's motives: "Out on spec probably" (13. 808). As an advertising canvasser, Bloom would certainly be aware of consumer habits, and his comment on how to attract female customers is telling: "Best place for an ad to catch a woman's eye on a mirror" (13.919–20). Commenting on Gerty, Thomas Karr Richards has noted, "no other character in *Ulysses* can be so summarily pigeonholed; yet no other's discourse in *Ulysses* is so much the product, not of an exclusive persona, but of the collective pressure of the customs and ideology of a burgeoning consumer society" (755).

But the issues are more sexual than commercial, to whatever extent the two can be separated here. When a woman looks, Doane claims that the dynamics differ from those of a man's gaze: "The woman's sexuality, as spectator, must undergo a constant process of transformation. She must look, as if she were a man with the phallic power of the gaze, in order to be that woman," the one imaged (199). Gerty often assumes this look in her portion of the episode; she presumes (and quite rightly) to know what Bloom is looking at and what his reaction will be: "Three and eleven she paid for those stockings . . . and that was what he was looking at, transparent, and not at her [Cissy's] insignificant ones that had neither shape nor form (the cheek of her!) because he had eyes in his head to see the difference for himself" (13.499–504). And in the episode's (and probably the novel's) most oft-read scene, Gerty's assumption of Bloom's look is evident from the content and the style of the prose:

> She leaned back far to look up where the fireworks were and she caught her knee in her hands so as not to fall back looking up and there was no-one to see only him and her when she revealed all her graceful beautifully shaped legs like that, supply soft and delicately rounded and she seemed to hear the panting of his heart, his hoarse breathing, because she knew too about the passion of men like that, hotblooded. . . (13.695–700)

She regards her legs as he would and chronicles the effect that she would have on herself were she a man, concluding in rhetoric reminiscent of *Sweets of Sin*. As Gerty pores over her magazines, as she plans her wardrobe, she assumes the phallic power of the gaze: "and to possess the image," Doane writes, "through the gaze is to become it" (199). This collapsing of image and self can happen even in the outhouse, or "that place" as Gerty genteelly prefers to call it:

> tacked up on the wall of that place . . . the picture of halcyon days where a young gentleman . . . was offering a bunch of flowers to his ladylove with oldtime chivalry through her lattice window. . . . She was in a soft clinging white in a studied attitude. . . . [Gerty] often looked at them dreamily . . . and felt *her own arms* that were white and soft *just like hers* with the sleeves back. . . (13.334–44; emphasis added)

And, of course, such melding of image and self frequently occurs in the privacy of the boudoir: "She did it [her hat] all by herself and what joy was hers when she tried it on then, smiling at the lovely reflection which the mirror gave back to her!" (13.162). She is pleased because she finds herself attractive; i.e., she believes that men will find her appearance enticing. When she judges herself, she regards herself as if she were a man looking at a woman and she assesses the image accordingly. "Binding identification to desire (the basic strategy of narcissism), the teleological aim of the female look demands a becoming and hence, a dispossession. She must give up the image to become it," unlike the male (Doane 199).

According to Doane this "becoming" represents a masquerade which, as she argues in "Film and the Masquerade: Theorising the Female Spectator": "constitutes an acknowledgment that it is femininity itself which is constructed as mask—as the decorative layer which conceals a non-identity." She quotes from the work of the psychoanalyst, Joan Riviere, "the first to theorise the concept":

> Womanliness therefore could be assumed and worn as a mask, both to hide the possession of masculinity [for example, Gerty's appropriation of the male sexualized gaze] and to avert the reprisals expected if she was found to possess it. . . . The reader may now ask how I define womanliness or where I draw the line between genuine womanliness and the masquerade. My suggestion is not, however, that there is any such difference; whether radical or superficial, they are the same thing. (81)4

Gerty's decorative layer of femininity conceals her non-identity, the impossibility of complete acceptance for a lame young woman in a culture unwilling to acknowledge her as a full participating member. Gerty attempts to mask her flaw: "but for that one shortcoming she knew she need fear no competition and that was an accident coming down Dalkey Hill and she always tried to conceal it" (13.649–651). She shields herself behind the façade of "a womanly woman not like other flighty girls unfeminine he [Bloom] had known" (13.435). Assuming the masquerade as compensation for her lameness, she also uses it as a means to create desire in the male. In Lacan's words, the masquerade is "the feminine sexual attitude," a position taken up by all women (193). As Stephen Heath summarizes it: "Adornment *is* the woman, she exists veiled; only thus can she represent lack, be what is wanted: lack 'is never presented other than as a reflection on a veil'" (52). Gerty is, after all, "dressed up to the nines," a probable corruption of the phrase "dressed to then eyne" ("to the eyes"), that is, veiled (Brewer, "Nine"). Donned by Muslim women to thwart the male gaze, the veil in fact increases desire—as Roland Barthes asks, "Is not the most erotic portion of a body *where the garment gapes?*" (9)

Although Gerty has assumed the masquerade and become what men want her to be, in doing so she has gained power over men—she is fully conscious of her feminine desirability. By occasionally making eye contact with Bloom and moving just so, she succeeds in her efforts to inflame his passion for her: "perhaps he could see the bright steel buckles of her shoes if she swung them like that thoughtfully with the toes down" and "Gerty just took off her hat for a moment to settle her hair and a prettier, a daintier head of nutbrown tresses was never seen on a girl's shoulders . . . almost maddening in its sweetness" (13.424–5, 509–12). While Bloom's ejaculation confirms his masculinity, it also represents a victory for Gerty, a testament to her calculated charm.

Yet, her final response to their encounter is entirely consistent with her assuming a demeaning role as a creature subordinate to men. Gerty looks at Bloom with "an infinite store of mercy in those eyes, for him too a word of pardon even though he had erred and sinned and wandered. Should a girl tell? No, a thousand times no. That was their secret" (13.748–50). Even though Gerty encouraged Bloom's passion, one might expect her to be somewhat surprised at his public masturbation. Instead, she accepts his transgression quite naturally, gracefully forgives him and even promises to keep the incident a secret. In Gerty, Joyce created a woman who is everything that a man like Bloom could desire.

Within "women's" films, Doane notices a fiction of female subjectivity, a conceit exposed by a subsequent suspension of the female protagonist's narration. "The interruption of the filmic flow of images within the diegesis, . . . [in *Caught*] as in *Rebecca*, is the metaphor for the disintegration of a short-lived family romance. Spectator of a cinema whose parameters are defined as masculine, Leonora is dispossessed of both look and voice" (202). After Gerty performs her final, passive role of the feminine forgiver to the active, male transgressor, Bloom's portion of the episode begins, abruptly concluding Gerty's narrative and destroying her "short-lived family romance." Bloom's perspective is reasserted for the remainder of the chapter, dispossessing Gerty of her voice. With "Nausicaa," as with the "women's" pictures, "there is a sense . . . in which . . . [we] begin with a hypothesis of female subjectivity which is subsequently disproven by the textual project. . . . The films thus chronicle the emergence and disappearance of female subjectivity, the articulation of an 'I' which is subsequently negated" (213–14). The "woman's" episode of *Ulysses* shows us the emergence of woman as subject with the entrance into Gerty's stream-of-consciousness, but it also emphasizes repeatedly her status as object. "Nausicaa," like the "woman's" film, seeks "in some way to trace female subjectivity and desire," but really only offers the female from the male's perspective (196). It is but the first of the novel's attempts to explore the female psyche, through the eyes of a "winsome Irish" lass, but ultimately, of course, from the perspective of a male author and a male protagonist.

Finally, both Gerty's right to use her feminine power and her position as a female spectator are denied. When Bloom realizes that Gerty is lame, he regards her as a "curiosity like a nun or a negress" and compares her to that cliché that Dorothy Parker made famous in her couplet "News Item": "a girl with glasses" (13.776–77). As a flawed woman, Gerty is not quite deserving of male attention, and therefore her enticement of men through feminine charm becomes an act of deception. Indeed, Bloom is grateful that he didn't know the truth about her: "Glad I didn't know it when she was on show." (13.775–6) By daring to look at Bloom in a sexual manner, Gerty has appropriated the masculinized gaze, and "in usurping the gaze she poses a threat to an entire system of representation" (Doane, 83). Her replacement by Bloom's narrative reasserts the male dominance over her and the narrative itself—Gerty never completely rises above the level of spectacle, and her power, even in this realm, is hampered by her defect, her lameness. She momentarily assumes the position of spectator but is returned, or reduced, to spectacle throughout the episode; later, Bloom in "Circe," characterizes her spectating with demeaning descriptions like "leering" and "ogling," thereby suggesting he believes her to have trespassed on man's privilege (15.372–73). His own voyeurism, on the other hand, is denied ("I never saw you") in response to Gerty's accusation in the court of conscience that the episode becomes (15.378).

That Joyce is looking at the mysteries and implications of commercial female beauty, while assuming the conventions and psychology of romance novels and journals, is perfectly expressed in the narrator's matter-of-fact answer to a usually rapturous and rhetorical question: "Why have women such eyes of witchery?" (13.107). The romantic question set against its prosaic response, describing how such cosmetic effects are achieved, suggests the deflation of the popular genre as well as the demystification of "women's" dark and dangerous secrets. In 1931 Adrienne Monnier hinted at many of the aspects of "Nausicaa" I have discussed in this essay. The episode, she notes,

> up to Bloom's final monologue, preserves the tone of the articles and famous little announcements of fashion magazines. Everything that the ordinary woman places at her own feet, the whole flattering murmur that a crowd of others like herself produces in her, all the beauty advice, the dictates of fashion, the insipid poetry, the tame mystery, all-purpose religion, recipes, etiquette, and, hovering over all, impregnating the least detail, love like the atmosphere—yes everything is there; that devil of a Joyce has left out nothing. The masculine public keenly enjoyed this chapter.[5] (118)

And, as Monnier points out, Joyce has proceeded beyond those beauty secrets to an exploration of the psyche and gender roles created by this press. With the epithet, "that devil of a Joyce," she acknowledges that the author has invaded the forbidden territory of the "ordinary" woman. But men enjoyed it precisely because it presents a male view of females, all the while purporting to be a glimpse into female subjectivity—both Monnier's cynical description and her use of the adjective "ordinary" suggest her critique of this constructed view of women. Analysis utilizing feminist film theory encourages an investigation of sex roles within this "women's" world, explicating and revealing its agenda. Concurrently, Joyce has portrayed the fetishization and the demystification of woman, and shown us the responses of Gerty and Bloom to such a world view. When assessed through the theories of Mulvey and Doane, the visual pleasures of "Nausicaa" are revealed as mechanisms by which men have controlled women and reinforced the patriarchal order through various media.

NOTES

[1] Kimberly J. Devlin in "The Female Eye: Joyce's Voyeuristic Narcissists," also considers issues of scopophilia and voyeurism in this episode, but with a different focus. See Bonnie Kime Scott, ed., *New Alliances in Joyce Studies* (Newark: U of Delaware P, 1988), 135–43.

[2] The female reader/audience will be discussed. See pp. 88–95.

[3] Austin Briggs has identified both Peeping Tom and Willie's Hat as voyeuristic mutoscope productions from 1901 and 1897, respectively. He also speculates on a cinematic source for Bloom's hosiery fantasy. (See his article, pp. 146–48).

[4] It should be noted that Doane's "analysis of the concept of masquerade differs markedly from that of Luce Irigaray. . . . It also diverges to a great extent from the very important analysis of masquerade presented by Claire Johnston in `Femininity and the Masquerade: Anne of the Indies,' *Jacques Tourneur* London, British Film Institute, 1975, pp. 36–44." (See Doane, p. 81.)

To clarify the concept of the male sexualized gaze, one can also turn to Doane. Either gender looking represents a male gaze: "After all, even if it is admitted that the woman is frequently the object of the voyeuristic or fetishistic gaze in the cinema, what is there to prevent her from reversing the relation and appropriating the gaze for her own pleasure? Precisely the fact that the reversal itself remains locked within the same logic. The male striptease, the gigolo—both inevitably signify the mechanism of reversal itself, constituting themselves as aberrations whose acknowledgment simply reinforces the dominant system of aligning the sexual difference with a subject/object dichotomy. And *an essential attribute of that dominant system is the matching of male subjectivity with the agency of the look*" (Emphasis added; see Doane, p. 77).

[5] See also Bonnie Kime Scott, *Joyce and Feminism* (Bloomington: Indiana Univ. Press, 1984), pp. 102–103.

CONCLUSION
From Film and Literature to Movies and Modernism

> I was doing what the cinema was doing, I was making a continuous statement of what that person was until I had not many things but one thing. . . .
>
> I, of course did not think of it in terms of the cinema, in fact I doubt whether at that time I had ever seen a cinema but, and I cannot repeat this too often any one is of one's period and this our period was undoubtedly the period of the cinema. . . . And each of us in our own way are bound to express what the world in which we are living is doing.
>
> —Gertrude Stein, "Portraits and Repetition"

Too often the relationship between literature and cinema is limited to the connection between the original text and its adaptation to the screen; be it from the perspective of the screenwriter, the academic or the movie critic, the investigation usually centers on whether the film renders the literary text faithfully. Dudley Andrew argues for a broader consideration of the issues of adaptation in his essay, "The Well-Worn Muse: Adaptation in Film History and Theory," suggesting that the process of adapting is common in many arts and he categorizes various types. In the mode of adaptation that he delineates as "borrowing" he notes: "Here the artist employs, more or less extensively, the material idea or form of an earlier, generally successful text. Medieval paintings featuring biblical iconography and miracle plays based on Bible stories draw on an exceptional text whose power they borrow" (10). Indeed, he asserts that the issues concerned in "the study of adaptation . . . [are] logically tantamount to the study of the cinema as a whole" (14).

In the same manner, Joyce draws on much of literary tradition; similarly a consideration of the relationship between his art and the cinema can lead to a study of his whole canon, the beginnings of which I have offered here. As with both adaptations of and allusions to literature, a certain intertextuality exists between the cinema and modern literature which requires more extensive study. As I have demonstrated here, approaches to an analysis of this intertextuality include both film history and theory. Both of these fields can assist the critic in understanding and assessing modern literature—critical film theory, aesthetics and the developments of early film need to be included in our critical discussions as they form part of Joyce's world and inform his work.

Joyce and the other modernists experienced a revolution in perception that arrived contemporaneously with the advent of the cinema; certainly the movies played a role in the shaping of their experience of the world and, as the words of Gertrude Stein quoted above suggest, their means of expression. How the cinema, that melding of art and technology, has affected, influenced, and interacted with Joyce's novel has been suggested in these pages. The works of other modernists deserve similar exploration. While the prose fiction of Faulkner and Dos Passos have been examined in connection with the cinema, other modernists on both sides of the Atlantic merit similar exploration: Pound and Eliot, Woolf and Stein, Djuna Barnes and Lawrence Durrell might all be fruitfully examined in connection with the arrival of the cinema and the development of its devices.

As we begin to hear of the effects on perception stemming from the ubiquity of computers and the role of the user alters with the introduction and improvement of digital photography, interactive video, hypertext environments and virtual reality, we need to remind ourselves of the relationship between the modernists and their technologies. Further consideration of the effect of the cinematograph and its avatars will help us to understand a world in which a mechanical device made magic and transformed the way people viewed the world, at a time when a mouse was still a rodent and windows had not yet become an operating system.

To truly become Joyce's contemporaries and his interpreters, we must reenter his world, a world that witnessed the birth and maturation of the silent cinema and the emergence of the sound film. At the end of *Joyce, Bakhtin and Popular Literature*, R. B. Kershner writes that his analysis reinserts "the man's writing, protagonists, and—we must suppose—Joyce himself into history. As Bakhtin asserts, 'Literature is an inseparable part of the totality of culture and cannot be studied outside the total cultural context'" (297). We must locate the place of the cinema in the history of the modernists and grant the movies their rightful status in the cultural matrix that informs and frames the fiction of James Joyce.

Bibliography

Andrew, Dudley. "The Well-Worn Muse: Adaptation in Film History and Theory" in *Narrative Strategies: Original Essays in Film and Prose Fiction*. An Essays in Literature Book. Eds. Syndy M. Conger and Janice R. Welsch. Macomb: Western Illinois U, 1980.

Barnouw, Erik. *The Magician and the Cinema*. New York: Oxford UP, 1981.

Barrow, Craig Wallace. *Montage in James Joyce's* Ulysses. [Madrid]: Studia Humanitatis, 1980.

Barthes, Roland. *The Pleasure of the Text*. Trans. Richard Miller. New York: Hill, 1975.

Bazargan, Susan. "The Headings in 'Aeolus': A Cinematographic View." *James Joyce Quarterly.* 23 (1986): 345–50.

Bazin, Andrè. *What is Cinema?* 2 vols. Ed. and trans. Hugh Gray. Berkeley: U of California P, 1971.

Beach, Joseph Warren. *The Twentieth Century Novel: Studies in Technique*. New York: Appleton-Century, 1932.

Benjamin, Walter. "The Work of Art in the Age of Mechanical Reproduction." *Illuminations*. Ed., with an introduction by Hannah Arendt. Trans. by Harry Zohn. 1968. New York: Shocken Books, 1968. 217–51.

Bergstrom, Janet. "Enunciation and Sexual Difference." *Camera Obscura*, #3–4 (Summer, 1979), 33–70. Rpt. in *Feminism and Film Theory*. Ed. Constance Penley. New York: Routledge, 1988. 159–85.

Bordwell, David. "*Citizen Kane.*" *Film Comment*, Summer 1971, 7, #2, 38–47.

Brewer, E. Cobham. *Brewer's Dictionary of Phrase and Fable, Centenary Edition*. Revised by Ivor H. Evans. New York: Harper & Row, 1970.

Briggs, Austin. " 'Roll Away the Reel World, the Reel World': 'Circe' and Cinema." *Coping With Joyce: Essays from the Copenhagen Symposium*. Eds. Morris Beja and Shari Benstock. Columbus: Ohio State University, 1989. 145–56.

Brown, Homer Obed. *James Joyce's Early Fiction: The Biography of a Form*. Hamden, Connecticut: Archon-Shoe String Press, 1975.

Budgen, Frank. *James Joyce and the Making of* Ulysses. Bloomington: Indiana UP, 1960.

Calder-Marshall, Arthur. *The Innocent Eye: The Life of Robert J. Flaherty*. Based on research material by Paul Rotha and Basil Wright. New York: Harcourt, 1963.

Callaghan, Morley. *That Summer in Paris: Memories of Tangled Friendships with Hemingway, Fitzgerald and Some Others*. New York: Coward-McCann, 1963.

Cohen, Keith. *Film and Fiction: The Dynamics of Exchange*. New Haven: Yale UP, 1979.

Colum, Mary and Padraic. *Our Friend James Joyce*. Garden City, New York: Doubleday, 1958.

Costanzo, William V. "Joyce and Eisenstein: Literary Reflections on the Reel World." *Journal of Modern Literature*. 11 (1984): 175–80.

Croce, Benedetto. *Aesthetics as Science of Expression and Gener al Linguistic*. Trans. Douglas Ainslie, 1909. Rpt. in *Critical Theory Since*

Plato, pp. 726–735. Ed. Hazard Adams. New York: Harcourt, 1971.

Deane, Paul. "Motion Picture Technique in James Joyce's 'The Dead.'" *James Joyce Quarterly*. 6 (1969): 231–36.

Deming, Robert H., ed. *James Joyce: The Critical Heritage*. Vol. I: 1902–1927. New York: Barnes & Noble, 1970.

Devlin, Kimberly J. "The Female Eye: Joyce's Voyeuristic Narcissists." *New Alliances in Joyce Studies*. Ed. Bonnie Kime Scott. Newark: U of Delaware P, 1988. 135–43.

Doane, Mary Ann. "Caught and Rebecca: The Inscription of Femininity as Absence." *Enclitic* 5–6, #1–2 (Fall 1981–Spring 1982) 175–89. Rpt. in *Feminism and Film Theory*. Ed. Constance Penley. New York: Routledge, 1988. 196–215.

_____. "Film and the Masquerade: Theorising the Female Spectator." *Screen* 23, #3–4 (September–October 1982) 74–87.

Eisenstein, Sergei. *Film Form: Essays in Film Theory*. Ed. and trans. Jay Leyda. New York: Harcourt Brace Jovanovich, 1949.

_____. *The Film Sense*. Ed. and trans. by Jay Leyda. New York: Harcourt Brace Jovanovich, 1947.

_____. *Immoral Memories: An Autobiography*. Trans. Herbert Marshall. Boston: Houghton, 1983.

Ellmann, Richard. *James Joyce, New and Revised Edition*. New York: Oxford UP, 1982.

Flaubert, Gustave. *The Temptation of Saint Anthony*. Trans. Kitty Mrosovsky. Ithaca: Cornell UP, 1981.

Gifford, Don. Ulysses *Annotated: Notes for James Joyce's Ulysses*. Rev. ed. With Robert J. Seidman. Berkeley: U California P, 1988.

Gilbert, Sandra M. "Sonnet: The Ladies' Home Journal" in *Emily's Bread: Poems*. New York: Norton, 1984.

Glasheen, Adaline. *Third Census of Finnegans Wake: An Index of the Characters and their Roles*. Berkeley and Los Angeles: U California P, 1977.

Goethe, Johann Wolfgang von. *Faust*. Part One and Sections from Part Two. Trans. by Walter Kaufmann. New York: Anchor-Doubleday, 1961.

Gonzales, Deborah Martin. "'Drauma' and 'Newseryreel': Joyce's Dramatic Aesthetic in Adaptation." *DAI* 47 (1987): 2594A. Tulane U.

Grierson, John. "First Principles of Documentary." *Cinema Quarterly*: Winter 1932, Spring 1933, Spring 1934. Rpt. in *Grierson on Documentary*, pp. 145–56. Ed. and compiled by Forsyth Hardy. New York: Praeger, 1971.

Hauser, Arnold. *The Social History of Art*. 2 vols. Trans. in collaboration with the author by Stanley Godman. New York: Knopf, 1952.

Heath, Stephen. "Joan Riviere and the Masquerade." *Formations of Fantasy*. Eds. Victor Burgin, James Donald and Cora Kaplan. New York: Methuen, 1986. 45–61.

Humphrey, Robert. *Stream of Consciousness in the Modern Novel*. Perspectives in Criticism 3. Berkeley and Los Angeles: U California P, 1955.

Hutchins, Patricia. "James Joyce and the Cinema." *Sight and Sound*. 21 (1951): 9–12.

_____. *James Joyce's World*. London: Methuen, 1957.

Joyce, James. "Aesthetics," in *The Critical Writings*. Ed. by Ellsworth Mason and Richard Ellmann. New York: Viking, 1959. 141–48.

_____. "Drama and Life," in *The Critical Writings*. Ed. by Ellsworth Mason and Richard Ellmann. New York: Viking, 1959. 38–46.

_____. *Dubliners*. Ed. By Robert Scholes and A. Walton Litz. 1916; New York: Viking, 1969.

———. *Finnegans Wake*. 1939; New York: Viking, 1958. Eighth printing with the author's corrections incorporated in the text.

———. *James Joyce's Scribbledehobble: The Ur-Workbook for* Finnegans Wake. Ed., with notes and an introduction by Thomas E. Connolly. [Evanston, Illinois]: Northwestern UP, 1961.

———. *Letters*. Eds. Stuart Gilbert, vol.1; Richard Ellmann, vols. 2–3. New York: Viking, 1966.

———. *A Portrait of the Artist as a Young Man*. 1916; New York: Viking, 1968.

———. "A Portrait of the Artist." Ed. Richard M. Kain and Robert Scholes. *Yale Review*, XLIX (Spring 1960): 355–69. Rpt. in *A Portrait of the Artist as a Young Man*. Viking Critical Edition. Ed. Chester G. Anderson. New York: Penguin, 1977. 257–66.

———. *Stephen Hero*. Ed. by Theodore Spencer, John J. Slocum and Herbert Cahoon. New York: New Directions, 1963.

———. *Ulysses*. Ed. by Hans Walter Gabler, et al. 1922; New York: Random House, 1986.

Joyce, Stanislaus. *My Brother's Keeper: James Joyce's Early Years*. New York: Viking Press, 1958.

Katz, Ephraim. *The Film Encyclopedia*. New York: Putnam, 1979. "Documentary."

Kenner, Hugh. *The Mechanic Muse*. New York: Oxford UP, 1978.

———. *The Pound Era*. Berkeley: U California P, 1971.

———. *Ulysses* London: Allen & Unwin, 1980.

Kershner, R. B. *Joyce, Bakhtin, and Popular Literature: Chronicles of Disorder*. Chapel Hill: U of North Carolina P, 1989.

Kracauer, Siegfried. *Theory of Film: The Redemption of Physical Reality*. New York: Oxford UP, 1960.

Kristeva, Julia. *Revolution in Poetic Language*. Trans. Margaret Waller. New York: Columbia UP, 1984.

Lacan, Jacques. *The Four Fundamental Concepts of Psycho-Analysis*. Ed. Jacques-Alain Miller. Trans. Alan Sheridan. New York: Norton, 1978.

Levin, Harry. *James Joyce: A Critical Introduction, Revised and Augmented Edition*. Norfolk, Connecticut: New Directions Books, 1960.

Lindsay, Vachel. *The Art of the Moving Picture*. Revised ed. 1922; New York: Liveright, 1970.

Lukács, Georg. *Studies in European Realism*. London: Merlin Press, 1972.

Magalaner, Marvin. *Time of Apprenticeship: The Fiction of Young James Joyce*. New York: Abelard-Schuman, 1959.

Mast, Gerald. *A Short History of the Movies*. 2nd ed. Indianapolis: Bobbs, 1976.

McHugh, Roland. *Annotations to Finnegans Wake*. London: Routledge and Kegan Paul, 1980.

McLuhan, Marshall. *Understanding Media: The Extensions of Man*. New York: McGraw, 1964.

Minden, Michael. "The City in Early Cinema: Metropolis, Berlin, and October." In *Unreal City: Urban Experience in Modern European Literature and Art*. Ed. by Edward Timms and David Kelley. Manchester: Manchester UP, 1985. 193–213.

Modleski, Tania. *The Women Who Knew Too Much: Hitchcock and Feminist Theory*. New York: Methuen, 1988.

Monnier, Adrienne. "Joyce's Ulysses and the French Public." *The Very Rich Hours of Adrienne Monnier*. Ed. and Trans. Richard Mc Dougall. New York: Scribner's, 1976. 112–126.

Moussinac, Lèon. *Sergei Michaelovich Eisenstein*. Paris: Editions Seghers,

1964. Quoted and translated in Joseph Evans Slate, "The Reisman-Zukofsy Screenplay of Ulysses: Its Background and Significance," *Library Chronicle of the University of Texas,* (1982) 106–39.

Mulvey, Laura. "Afterthoughts on 'Visual Pleasure and Narrative Cinema' inspired by *Duel in the Sun.*" Framework 6, #15–17 (1981) 12–15. Rpt. in *Feminism and Film Theory*. Ed. Constance Penley. New York: Routledge, 1988. 69–79.

_____. "Visual Pleasure and Narrative Cinema." Screen 16, #3 (Autumn, 1975) 6–18. Rpt. in *Feminism and Film Theory*. Ed. Constance Penley. New York: Routledge, 1988. 57–68.

Murray, Edward. *The Cinematic Imagination: Writers and the Motion Pictures*. New York: Frederick Ungar, 1972.

Nabokov, Vladimir. *Lectures on Literature*. Ed. by Fredson Bowers. New York: Harcourt, 1980.

Noel, Lucie. *James Joyce and Paul L. Lèon: The Story of A Friendship*. New York: Gotham Book Mart, 1950.

Palmer, R. Barton. "Eisensteinian Montage and Joyce's *Ulysses*: The Analogy Reconsidered." *Mosaic*. 18 (1985): 73–85.

Parr, Mary. *James Joyce: The Poetry of Conscience, A Study of* Ulysses. Milwaukee: Inland Press, 1961.

Pearce, Richard. "Experimentation with the Grotesque: Comic Collisions in the Grotesque World of *Ulysses*." *Modern Fiction Studies*. 20 (1974): 378–84.

_____. *The Novel in Motion: An Approach to Modern Fiction*. Columbus: Ohio State UP, 1983.

Perlmutter, Ruth. "Joyce and Cinema." *Boundary 2*. 6 (1978): 481–502.

Pound, Ezra. "The Editor: Data." *The Exile*, Autumn 1928.

_____. *Literary Essays of Ezra Pound*. Ed. and with an introduction by T. S. Eliot. London: Faber and Faber, 1954.

Potts, Willard, ed. *Portraits of the Artist in Exile: Recollec tions of James Joyce by Europeans* New York: Harcourt, 1986; reprint of Seattle: U Washington Press, 1979.

Power, Arthur. *Conversations with James Joyce*. Ed. by Clive Hart. London: Millington, 1974.

Richards, Thomas Karr. "Gerty MacDowell and the Irish Common Reader." *ELH* 52, #3 (Fall, 1985): 755–776.

Ryf, Robert S. *A New Approach to Joyce:* The Portrait of the Artist *as a Guidebook*. Berkeley: U California P, 1962.

Seton, Marie. *Sergei M. Eisenstein: A Biography*. New York: Grove Press, 1960.

Slate, Joseph Evans. "The Reisman-Zukofsky Screenplay of *Ulysses*: Its Background and Significance." *Library Chronicle of the University of Texas*, 1982: 106–39.

Smith, Samuel. *My Life-Work*. London: Hodder and Stoughton, 1902.

Sontag, Susan. *On Photography*. New York: Farrar, 1977.

Spiegel, Alan. *Fiction and the Camera Eye: Visual Consciousness in Film and the Modern Novel*. Charlottesville: UP of Virginia, 1976.

Steinberg, Erwin. *The Stream of Consciousness and Beyond in* Ulysses. Pittsburgh: U Pittsburgh P, 1972.

Strindberg, August. *Plays: Two*. Trans. with an introduction by Michael Meyer. London: Methuen, 1982.

Thornton, Weldon. *Allusions in* Ulysses. Chapel Hill: U North Carolina P, 1968.

Tindall, William York. *A Reader's Guide to* Finnegans Wake. New York: Farrar, 1969.

Wakeman, John, ed. *World Film Directors*. Vol. 1: 1890–1945. New York:

H. W. Wilson, 1987.

Watt, Ian. *The Rise of the Novel*. Berkeley: U of California P, 1957.

Werner, Gösta. "James Joyce, Manager of the First Cinema in Ireland." *Nordic Rejoycings, 1982, in commemoration of the centenary of the birth of James Joyce*. Stockholm: The James Joyce Society of Sweden and Finland, 1982. 125-36.

———. "James Joyce and Sergej Eisenstein." Trans. Erik Gunnemark. *James Joyce Quarterly*. 27 (1990): 491-507.

Wilde, Oscar. "The Decay of Lying" in *Oscar Wilde*. Ed. by Isobel Murray. New York: Oxford UP, 1989. 215-239.

Index

adaptation, 99–100
Andrew, Dudley, 99–100
artifice, in cinema, 31

Bakhtin, Mikhail, 101
Barrow, Craig Wallace, 13–14
Battleship Potemkin, 28. *See also* Eisenstein, Sergei
Bazargan, Susan, 16
Bazin, André, xiii, xiv, 31, 35, 38–41
Beach, Joseph Warren, 8
Benjamin, Walter, xiv, 20, 21–22, 29
Bergson, Henri, xiv, 24
Berlin, xiii, 41–46. *See also* Walther Ruttmann
Bitzer, Billy, 65, 68
Bordwell, David, 31–32
Briggs, Austin, xiv, 2, 16, 72, 96n
Brown, Homer Obed , 2
Bute, Mary Ellen, 11

Callaghan, Morley, 4–5
castration anxiety, 83
Chaplin, Charlie, 9, 74, 80n
cinema
    and the city, 45–46
    and eroticism, 6
    and external reality, 22, 31
    and fantasy, 65
    and the psyche, 22
    and magic, 69–72
    and mimesis, 8, 36
    and subjectivity, 8
cinematic devices in literature, 8–9, 23
Citizen Kane, 31–32
Cohen, Keith, xi, 13
Colum, Mary, 6
Conrad, Joseph, 11
Costanzo, William V., 14–15, 50–52
Croce, Benedetto, xiv, 36

dadaism, 22
Daguerre, Louis, 36
DeSica, Vittorio, 35
Deane, Paul, 10
Devlin, Kimberly J., 96n
Dietrich, Marlene, 6
Doane, Mary Ann, xiii, xv, 81–82, 88–94
documentary film, xiv, 37
dreams, compression of, 67
Dubliners, 37, 51
    individual stories:
        "Araby," 38, 39
        "The Boarding House," 34
        "Clay," 39
        "The Dead," 66
        "An Encounter," 35, 39

"Eveline," 38
"Grace," 23
"Ivy Day in the Committee Room," 41
"A Little Cloud," 40
"A Painful Case," 34
"The Sisters," 39, 66
"Two Gallants," 38

Eisenstein, Sergei:
   adaptation of *Ulysses* proposed, 7
   cinema of inner monologue, 2
   "The Cinematographic Principle and the Ideogram," 8, 9, 49
   deformation of images, xiii, 53–62
   dispropostion in representation, xiv
   Immoral Memories, 7, 62
   and Japanese art, 49
   and Japanese hieroglyph, 62
   on Joyce and cinematography, xii
   meeting with Joyce, 6–7, 16n
   and montage, xiii, xiv, 15, 28
   montage as conflict, 14, 52
   parallels to Joyce and Godard, 12–13
   word combinations, xiv, 50, 52
   "Word and Image," 52
Eisensteinian analysis of Joyce, 49–64
epiphany, 40. *See also Stephen Hero*

female spectator, 90–95
Feminist Film Theory, xv, 81–96
film editing, 21. *See also* Eisenstein, montage
Finnegans Wake, 26–27, 35, 41, 50, 67, 68
Flaherty, Robert, xiv, 5, 7, 33, 37–38
Flaubert, Gustav, 11–12, 36, 47n, 77–78
Frank, Nino, 5
Fregoli, Leopoldo, 65

Gilbert, Stuart, 7
Godard, Jean-Luc, 12–13
Goethe, Johann Wolfgang von, 77
Gonzales, Deborah Martin, 15–16

Grierson, John, 37
Griffith, D. W., 26, 27

haiku, 58
Hauser, Arnold, xiv, 13, 24–28
Heath, Stephen, 90
Herr, Cheryl, xiii
Humphrey, Robert, 8–9
Hutchins, Patricia, 4, 5

immanence, 41
intertextuality, xi, 100
James, Henry, 11, 32
Jolas, Eugene and Maria, 5, 7
Joyce, James
   compound words, 51
   Critical Writings, 36
   "Drama and Life," 33–35
   film adaptation proposals for *Ulysses* and *Finnegans Wake*, 7
   Letters, 3, 4, 35, 37–38, 50
   "A Portrait of the Artist" (1904 Essay), 2
   Scribbledehobble, 6, 79
   See also Dubliners, Finnegans Wake, A Portrait of the Artist as a Young Man, Stephen Hero, and *Ulysses*
Joyce, Stanislaus, 1–2, 34

Kenner, Hugh, xiv, 19–21, 53
Kershner, R. B., xiii, 100–01
Kolb, Jack, 63n
Kracauer, Siegfried, 42
Kristeva, Julia, xi
Kuleshov, Lev, 23

Lacan, Jacques, xv, 93
Lamarr, Hedy, 6
Leon, Paul, 7
Leslie, Shane, 23
Levin, Harry, xii, 8
Linder, Max, 74
Lindsay, Vachel, xiv, 65, 69, 72, 73, 74–76
Lloyd, Harold, 74

Index

Lukács, Georg, 35
Lumière, Louis and Auguste, xiv, 31–32, 35

McHugh, Roland, 63n
McLuhan, Marshall, 9–10

Man of Aran, 5, 37. See also Flaherty
masquerade, 88, 90, 92
Méliès, Georges, 10, 16n, 31–32, 65, 68–70, 80n
Metz, Christian, xi
Minden, Michael, 43–46
Moana, 37. See also Flaherty
Monnier, Adrienne, 95
Montage, xii, 2, 11, 51–53
Moussinac, Leon, xii
multiperspectivism, 46
Mulvey, Laura, xiii, xv, 81–88
Murray, Edward, 11

Nanook of the North, 37. See also Flaherty
narcissism, 82
Noel, Lucie, 6

Palmer, R. Barton, 15
Parr, Mary, 9, 63n
Pearce, Richard, 14
Perlmutter, Ruth, 12–13
phenomenology, 41
Portrait of the Artist as a Young Man, A, 37, 47n, 51–52, 55–56, 67
Pound, Ezra, 42
Power, Arthur, 34
protosurrealism, xiv, 65

realism in cinema, 31
Reisman, Jerry, 7
Reisman-Zukofsky scenario of *Ulysses*, 17n
Richards, Thomas Karr, 91
Riviere, Joan, xv, 90, 92
Rossellini, Roberto, 35, 40
Ruttmann, Walther, xiii, xiv, 7, 33, 41–46. See also Berlin
Ryf, Robert, 10, 16n, 63n

scopophilia, xv, 82, 84–85
Seton, Marie, 6
Sontag, Susan, xiv, 33, 36
spectator identification, 81
Spiegel, Alan, xi, 11–12
Spottiswoode, Raymond, 13–14
Stein, Gertrude, 99–100
Steinberg, Erwin, 63n
Stephen Hero, 28, 40, 43. See also epiphany
Strick, Joseph, 11
Strindberg, August, 78–79

technological innovations, 19–21
Tindall, William York, 10–11
Tolstoy, Leo, xi

Ulysses, 27, 41
  and compound words, 52
  deformation and disproportion, 56–62
  film adaptation, xiv
  film proposals, 7
  and Japanese poetry, 59
  Japanese translation, 49–50
  and Méliès, 68
  individual episodes:
    "Aeolus," 43, 45, 73
    "Calypso," 25, 26, 59–62
    "Circe," 52, 69–70, 72–79, 95
    "Cyclops," 33, 35, 82
    "Eumaeus," 84–85
    "Hades," 43, 70
    "Ithaca," 33
    "Lestrygonians," 28, 43, 70, 73
    "Lotus-Eaters," 29n, 84
    "Nausicaa," 29, 81–96
    "Oxen of the Sun," 53, 74, 76
    "Penelope," 26
    "Proteus," 25
    "Scylla and Charybdis," 53
    "Sirens," 25, 44, 74
    "Telemachus," 25, 26, 28, 52,

56–59, 71–72
"Wandering Rocks," 24, 33, 35, 74

Volta Cinematograph, 4, 45
voyeurism, xv, 2, 81, 82
voyeuristic demystification, 86

Warner Brothers, 7
Watt, Ian 32–33
Wells, H. G., 5
Welles, Orson, 31–32
Werner, Gösta, 4, 16n
Wilde, Oscar, 29
Woolf, Virginia, 9
Wyler, William, 5

Zola, Émile, 40
Zukofsky, Louis, 7